Contemporary Waterproofing Design

Detailing for
Multi-component Ultra Fast Curing Polyurethane
Waterproofing Membrane Systems

編集協力:赤松佳珠子(CAt), 須部恭浩(三菱地所設計), 多喜茂(日建設計)

アートディレクション+デザイン:塩谷嘉章

翻訳:ブライアン アムスタッツ, ブレインウッズ株式会社

Contributing Editors : Kazuko AKAMATSU (CAt), Yasuhiro SUBE (MITSUBISHI JISHO SEKKEI INC.), Shigeru TAKI (NIKKEN SEKKEI LTD)

Art Direction + Design : Yoshiaki SHIOYA

Translation : Brian Amstutz, Brainwoods Co., Ltd.

〈註〉
本書では、超速硬化ウレタンのみを用いた防水を超速硬化ウレタン防水と表記し、
手塗りウレタンや通気緩衝シートと超速硬化ウレタンとの複合防水を超速硬化ウレタン複合防水と表記する。

〈Note〉
In this publication, "ultra fast curing polyurethane waterproofing membrane" denotes waterproofing using only ultra fast curing polyurethane. Multi-component waterproofing using hand-applied urethane or breathable buffer sheet together with ultra fast curing urethane waterproofing is termed "multi-component ultra fast curing polyurethane waterproofing membrane."

防水デザインの現在

超速硬化ウレタン複合防水
とディテール

彰国社 編

防水は進化している。

水から人を守ること、言い換えれば、建物が漏水しないことは、建築が確保すべき性能の最も基本的な事柄の一つである。だからこそ防水種別の選定は重要であり、その性能を担保するためのディテールと、デザインとの間ではせめぎ合いが起こりがちだ。それらをうまく納められるかどうかに設計者の力量が問われる。

現在、建築に採用されている防水種別のシェアの上位を見ると、ウレタン防水が約3割、シート防水が約3割、アスファルト防水が約2割である（2017年日本防水材料連合会のデータより）。かつて防水の主流のように考えられていたアスファルト防水の比率が低下しつつある背景として、施工する職人不足などいくつかの理由が挙げられるが、注目すべきはウレタン防水の比率の高まりではないだろうか。

本書は、近年、建物の本防水として普及しつつある超速硬化ウレタン複合防水を用いた優れた建築とそのディテールを紹介するものである。

たとえば、超速硬化ウレタン複合防水では、アスファルト防水の陸屋根の基本納まりであるパラペットのアゴと一定の立上り高さ、そして防水層の保護材が不要となる。また、専用の機械で吹き付けるため、どのような形状や下地にも対応できる。基本的な高低と排水経路を押さえておけば、これまで防水との兼ね合いで必要だと考えられてきたさまざまなディテールが非常にシンプルにでき、デザインへの適応性も高い。

本書では、超速硬化ウレタン複合防水の基本的な考え方をはじめ、その納まりのバリエーションを21の事例として収録した。今後、超速硬化ウレタン複合防水を用いて設計するときのための定番書として、ぜひ手元に置いていただきたい。　　　　　　　　　　　———— 編集部

Waterproofing is evolving.

Protecting people from water, namely, maintaining a building which does not leak water is one of the most fundamental performances a building must ensure. Thus, selection of waterproofing material is very important and conflicts often occur between the design and the details ensuring the performances. Designer's competence for balancing them will be put to the test.

Looking at the major players of waterproofing materials which are currently in use for buildings, polyurethane waterproofing, sheet waterproofing and asphalt waterproofing account for approximately 30%, 30% and 20%, respectively (according to the 2017 data provided by the Japan Waterproofing Materials Association). While there are many backgrounds to the decrease of asphalt waterproofing which used to be considered as the mainstream waterproofing such as scarcity of engineers, the increase of the polyurethane waterproofing is remarkable.

This magazine introduces excellent buildings incorporating the Multi-component ultra fast curing polyurethane waterproofing membrane systems which has become increasingly popular as the mainstream building waterproofing in recent years and their details.

For instance, while asphalt waterproofing requires parapet corbel, fixed rise height and protection materials of a waterproof layer for its basic settlement of a flat roof, Multi-component ultra fast curing polyurethane waterproofing membrane systems requires none of these. Moreover, it can be used for any shape and foundation as it is sprayed with a special machine. By ensuring basic height and drainage, various details which had been considered necessary in balancing with waterproofing can be done simply and it is highly adjustable to various designs.

The magazine covers the fundamental philosophy of the Multi-component ultra fast curing polyurethane waterproofing membrane systems as well as its settlement variations as 21 examples. We hope that this magazine will be a standard reference for designing a building with the Multi-component ultra fast curing polyurethane waterproofing membrane systems in the future.

———— Editorial Department

部位からみる超速硬化ウレタン複合防水 ——— 8

教えて！超速硬化ウレタン複合防水Q&A ——— 11

超速硬化ウレタン複合防水のディテールポイント ——— 14

屋根・屋上 I（パラペット・緑化）
追手門学院大学 120周年記念プロジェクト　三菱地所設計 ——— 18
豊中市立文化芸術センター　日建設計 ——— 24
長崎県庁舎　日建設計，松林建築設計事務所，池田設計 ——— 28
立川市立第一小学校，柴崎図書館　小嶋一浩＋赤松佳珠子／CAt ——— 34

屋根・屋上 II（デッキ）
愛知県立愛知総合工科高等学校　久米設計 ——— 38
臺北南山廣場　三菱地所設計，瀚亞國際設計 ——— 42
W-place　三菱地所設計 ——— 48
竹中大工道具館新館　竹中工務店 ——— 52

曲面屋根
川口市めぐりの森　伊東豊雄建築設計事務所 ——— 56
アストラムライン新白島駅　小嶋一浩＋赤松佳珠子／CAt，パシフィックコンサルタンツ ——— 60
多治見市モザイクタイルミュージアム　藤森照信＋エイ・ケイ設計＋エース設計共同体 ——— 64
台中国家歌劇院　伊東豊雄建築設計事務所・大矩聯合建築師事務所 ——— 68

屋根＋外装
青森県立美術館　青木淳建築計画事務所 ——— 72
東北学院大学 土樋キャンパス ホーイ記念館　三菱地所設計 ——— 76
本郷台キリスト教会 チャーチスクール・保育園　保坂猛建築都市設計事務所／保坂猛 ——— 80

バルコニー
流山市立おおたかの森小・中学校　小嶋一浩＋赤松佳珠子／CAt ——— 84
大阪木材仲買会館　竹中工務店 ——— 88

庇
関西外国語大学 インターナショナルコミュニケーションセンター　日建設計 ——— 92
独立行政法人国立文化財機構 奈良文化財研究所　日本設計 ——— 96
新ダイビル　日建設計 ——— 100

プロジェクト
追手門学院大学 新キャンパス　三菱地所設計 ——— 104

鼎談
超速硬化ウレタン複合防水が建築デザインを変える　赤松佳珠子×須部恭浩×多喜茂 ——— 111

インタビュー
超速硬化ウレタン複合防水の現在　石川貴紀 ——— 120

Learning about
the Multi-component Ultra Fast Curing Polyurethane Waterproofing Membrane Systems from parts —— 8

Tell me! Q&A on
the Multi-component Ultra Fast Curing Polyurethane Waterproofing Membrane Systems —— 11

Detail Points on
the Multi-component Ultra Fast Curing Polyurethane Waterproofing Membrane Systems —— 14

Roof, Rooftop I – Parapet, Greening

Otemon Gakuin University 120th Anniversary Project   MITSUBISHI JISHO SEKKEI INC. —— 18

Toyonaka Performing Arts Center   NIKKEN SEKKEI LTD —— 24

Nagasaki Prefecture Office   NIKKEN SEKKEI LTD, MATSUBAYASHI ARCHITECTURAL DESIGN OFFICE, IKEDA ARCHITECTS —— 28

Tachikawa Daiichi Elementary School, Shibasaki Library   Kazuhiro Kojima + Kazuko Akamatsu / CAt —— 34

Roof, Rooftop II – Deck

Aichi High School of Technology and Engineering   KUME SEKKEI Co., Ltd. —— 38

Taipei Nanshan Plaza   MITSUBISHI JISHO SEKKEI INC., ARCHASIA DESIGN GROUP —— 42

W-place   MITSUBISHI JISHO SEKKEI INC. —— 48

Takenaka Carpentry Tools Museum   Takenaka Corporation —— 52

Curved Roof

'Meguri no Mori' Kawaguchi City Funeral Hall   Toyo Ito & Associates, Architects —— 56

Astramline Shin-hakushima Station   Kazuhiro Kojima + Kazuko Akamatsu / CAt, PACIFIC CONSULTANTS CO., LTD. —— 60

Mosaic Tile Museum, Tajimi   Terunobu Fujimori, Space Design Office ak-sekkei, Ace Design Comunity —— 64

National Taichung Theater   Toyo Ito & Associates, Architects, DA-JU Architects & Associates —— 68

Roof + Cladding

Aomori Museum of Art   JUN AOKI & ASSOCIATES —— 72

Tohoku Gakuin University Tsuchitoi Campus Hoy Memorial Hall   MITSUBISHI JISHO SEKKEI INC. —— 76

Hongodai Christcharch School & Nursery   TAKESHI HOSAKA ARCHITECTS / TAKESHI HOSAKA —— 80

Balcony

Nagareyama Otakanomori Elementary and Junior High School   Kazuhiro Kojima + Kazuko Akamatsu / CAt —— 84

Osaka Timber Association Building   Takenaka Corporation —— 88

Eaves

International Communication Center Kansai Gaidai University   NIKKEN SEKKEI LTD —— 92

Nara National Research Institute for Cultural Properties   NIHON SEKKEI, INC. —— 96

Shin-Daibiru Building   NIKKEN SEKKEI LTD —— 100

Project

Otemon Gakuin University New Campus   MITSUBISHI JISHO SEKKEI INC. —— 104

Round Table
Multi-component Ultra Fast Curing Polyurethane Waterproofing Membrane Systems
Will Change Architectural Design   Kazuko AKAMATSU × Yasuhiro SUBE × Shigeru TAKI —— 111

Interview
Current Status of
the Multi-component Ultra Fast Curing Polyurethane Waterproofing Membrane Systems   Takanori ISHIKAWA —— 120

部位からみる超速硬化ウレタン複合防水

テキスト：編集部 (P8-16)
Text : Editor (P8-16)

Learning about the Multi-component Ultra Fast Curing Polyurethane Waterproofing Membrane Systems from parts

超速硬化ウレタン複合防水の基本的な性能と納まりの考え方を主な部位ごとに見てみよう。

Let's look at the basic performance and detail concept of each major part of the Multi-component ultra fast curing polyurethane waterproofing membrane systems.

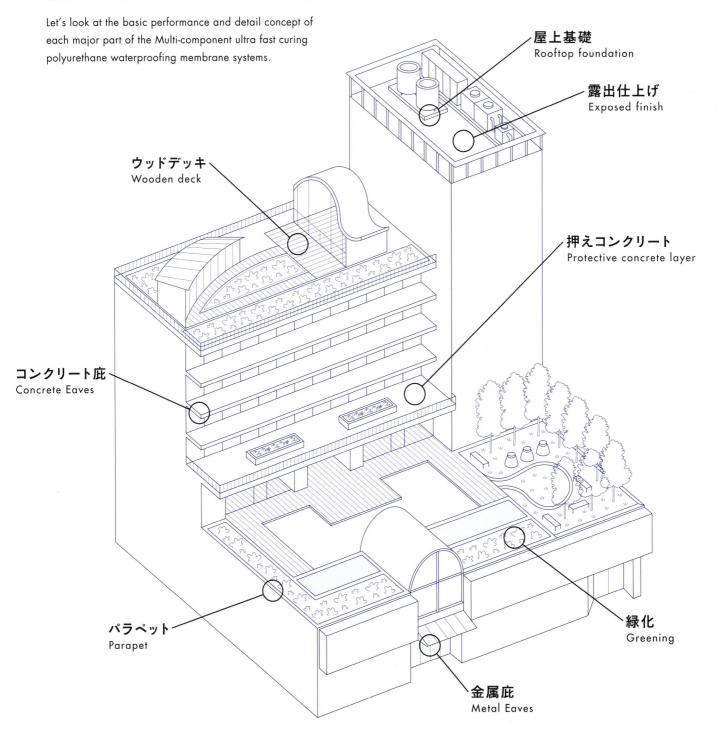

屋上基礎 / Rooftop foundation
露出仕上げ / Exposed finish
ウッドデッキ / Wooden deck
押えコンクリート / Protective concrete layer
コンクリート庇 / Concrete Eaves
パラペット / Parapet
緑化 / Greening
金属庇 / Metal Eaves

屋根・屋上 Roof, Rooftop

パラペット
Parapet

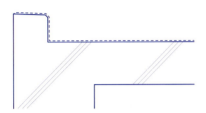

超速硬化ウレタンは、屋上床、パラペットの立上り、天端まで継目のない防水層を形成する。パラペットのアゴが不要で、納まりのための高さも必要ない。接着強度が高く、押え金物、笠木も不要。出隅は面取りが望ましい。

Ultra fast curing polyurethane waterproofing membrane system forms a seamless waterproof layer all the way up to the rooftop floor, parapet rise and levee crown. Parapet corbels are not required and height for settlement is also unnecessary. Neither flashing nor coping are needed with the high adhesive strength. Chamfering is desirable for the external corner.

緑化
Greening

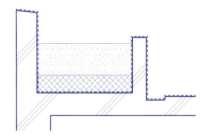

超速硬化ウレタンの一種であるポリウレアを使用すると、耐根性、耐薬品性も高くなり、耐根シートやモルタル等、耐根層の設置が不要。躯体に防水層を形成するだけで、直接緑化することができる。

The Ultra fast curing polyurethane waterproofing membrane system with high polyurea performance, the waterproof property, is excellent in root resistance and chemical resistance, and installation of anti-root layers such as anti-root mats and mortar is unnecessary. Greens can be placed directly on to the waterproof layer by simply forming a waterproof layer on top of a structure.

押えコンクリート
Protective concrete layer

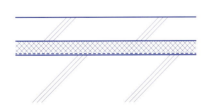

耐水性、耐アルカリ性に優れるため、防水層の上へ保護コンクリートを打設することが可能。主に、躯体の上に防水層を形成し、その上に外断熱層を設置、さらに保護コンクリートを打つような、外断熱歩行用途に採用される。

It can be used to pour protective concrete on top of a waterproof layer as it is excellent in water resistance and alkali resistance. It is used for external heat-insulating sidewalk where a protective concrete layer is poured after placing an external heat-insulating layer on top of a waterproof layer on a structure.

屋上基礎
Rooftop foundation

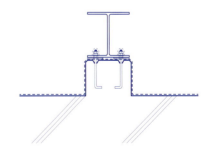

屋上に設ける架台の基礎でも、パラペット同様、アゴは不要となる。金属プレート、ボルトまわりの金属部分にも高い接着力を発揮するため、躯体から一体で防水層を形成し、水の浸入経路をつくらない。

Corbel is unnecessary just as parapet is, even for foundation for a frame which is to be installed on the rooftop. The high adhesive strength will form a uniform waterproof layer on a structure and prevent water from getting into metal plate and metal parts around bolts.

バルコニー Balcony

露出仕上げ
Exposed finish

超速硬化ウレタン防水は、一般歩行用途に対応しており、露出仕上げでは、厚みが薄く、軽量であることから、耐震性向上にも寄与する。歩行者の多い部位や、屋上駐車場なども露出仕上げにできる。

The Ultra fast curing polyurethane waterproofing membrane system can be used for concrete for sidewalk. With exposed finish, it contributes toward improvement of earthquake resistance as it is thin and light. Parts crossed over by many pedestrians and rooftop parking area can also be built with exposed finish.

ウッドデッキ
Wooden deck

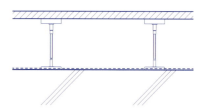

防水層自体が強靭なため、デッキの束は直接、接着処理で設置できる。サッシュとの取合いでは、アゴが不要なため室内外をフラットにしやすい。デッキの設置で紫外線カットの効果も得られ、防水膜の耐久性の向上にもなり得る。

Woods can be installed directly with adhesion treatment since the waterproof layer itself is very strong. It is easy to flatten the surrounding as sash arrangement does not require corbels. Deck can cut ultraviolet rays and can improve durability.

庇 Eaves

コンクリート
Concrete

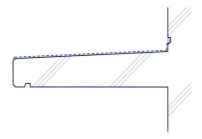

コンクリート庇を薄く仕上げるには最適な防水であり、長年使用され続けている。庇先端を水上にする場合にも、立上り高さが自由になり、薄く、軽量にできる。マットな質感の仕上げができるようにすることが今後の課題。

It is being used for many years as this waterproofing is suitable for finishing concrete eaves thin. Even when adjusting the edge of the eaves to be above water, it is perfect with its flexibility in wall height, thinness and light weight. It needs more improvement to enable matte finishes.

金属
Metal

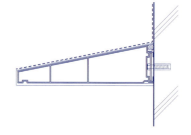

ほとんどの金属との接着がよく、壁面のコンクリートなど、他の素材とも一体で防水層を形成することができ、水の進入路をつくらない。庇だけでなく、丸環・水切り等、他の金属の設置物についても、同じように防水が容易である。

It adheres to most metals well and prevents water pathways with its ability to form a uniform waterproof layer with other materials such as wall concrete. Besides eaves, waterproofing of ring bolts, cutwater and other metal installations can be done easily in the same way.

教えて！
超速硬化ウレタン複合防水Q&A

Tell me! Q&A on the Multi-component Ultra Fast Curing
Polyurethane Waterproofing Membrane Systems

採用できる部位がイメージできたところで、超速硬化ウレタン複合防水の
さらに詳しい性質やメリットについて、Q&A形式で理解しよう。

Now that you have formed an image of the parts that can be used,
here are some Q&A's to help understand further details of the characteristics and benefits of
Multi-component ultra fast curing polyurethane waterproofing membrane systems.

Q そもそも「超速硬化ウレタン防水材」ってなに？
What is "Ultra fast curing polyurethane waterproofing material" in the first place?

A 硬化がとっても（超）速いウレタン防水材です。
A polyurethane waterproofing material which cures very（ultra）quickly.

ウレタン防水材は液体で、塗布後、化学反応によりゴム状に硬化します。一般的なウレタン防水材は手塗りで、硬化に1日程度要しますが、超速硬化ウレタン防水材は極めて硬化速度が速いため、専用吹付け機械で塗布し、均質で一体的な防水膜を形成します。

Polyurethane waterproofing material comes in a liquid form and becomes rubbery through a chemical reaction after it is spread. While it usually takes approximately one day for the regular polyurethane waterproofing material to cure, this Ultra fast curing polyurethane waterproofing material with extremely fast curing speed will form a homogenous, uniform waterproofing membrane when spread with a special spraying machine.

Q 「超速」ってどれくらい速いの？
How fast is "Ultra fast"?

A 約3分で硬くなります。
The material will cure in approximately 3 minutes.

主剤と硬化剤を撹拌してから3分程度で硬化してしまうため、手塗りでは対応できず、専用の吹付け機械で塗布します。塗布してから30秒以内に指触可能、3分以内に歩行可能になるため、垂直面でも流れ落ちることなく、どのような形状や勾配の下地でも対応できます。

Since the material will cure completely in approximately 3 minutes after mixing the main agent and the curative agent, it cannot be hand-coated and needs to be spread with a special spraying machine. The material will not run off and can be used for any shape and foundation with slope, as it can be hand-touched within 30 seconds of spreading and can be walked within 3 minutes.

Q 普通のウレタン防水（手塗ウレタン）となにが違うの？
How does it differ from regular polyurethane waterproofing material (hand-coating polyurethane)?

A 「硬化時間」「ゴム弾性性能」「耐水性」「伸張性」が違います。
"Curing time", "elasticity property of rubber", "water resistance" and "extensibility" are different.

硬化時間が極めて短いこと、また均質に塗布できることから、下地の形状や勾配を選ばないほか、ウレタンゴムの元々の性能であるゴム弾性性能によるクッション性がより高くなり、さらに硬さも増加しました。また、耐水性能も高くなり、水中でも使えます。

The extremely short curing time and the homogeneity allow the material to work any foundation shape or slope and have better hardness and cushioning property of rubber elasticity property which is the original property of polyurethane rubber. It can also be used underwater with better water resistance property.

Q 歩行用途には対応できる？
Can it be used for concrete for sidewalk?

A はい。露出仕上げで対応できます。
Yes, it can be used with exposed finish.

シート防水など、その他の防水材は、防水層の上に現場打ちコンクリートなどの保護層を設けて歩行用途に適応させますが、ウレタン防水材は、露出仕上げで歩行用途に対応できることが特徴です。屋上駐車場や大規模スポーツ施設など、重歩行にも対応可能です。

While sheet waterproofing material and other waterproofing materials are adjusted to be used for sidewalk concrete by placing a protective layer of cast-in-place concrete etc. on a waterproof layer, polyurethane waterproofing material is known for its adjustability with exposed aggregate finish. It can be used for rooftop parking area and large sports facility. Its surface hardness can hold heavy walking as well.

Q 池や屋上緑化に採用できる？
Can it be used for lakes and rooftop greening?

A はい。採用できます。
Yes, it can be.

超速硬化ウレタンの中でも、ポリウレア性能が高いものは、貯水池や屋上緑化、地下ピット、水中や地中の埋設構築物の防水にも適しています。上水施設の防水・防食のライニングにも使われています。防根性、防薬性も高く、屋上緑化でも保護層が必要ありません。

Materials with especially high polyurea among the Ultra fast curing polyurethane are suitable for waterproofing of reservoirs, rooftop greening, underground pits and underwater or underground-buried constructions. They are also used to line the waterproofing and anticorrosion of waterworks. With high root resistance and chemical resistance, protective layers are unnecessary even for rooftop greening.

Q 大面積でも大丈夫？
Can it be used for large area?

A 大面積も得意です！
Large area is the material's specialty!

面積を問わず適応します。吹付け後すぐに硬化し、歩行が可能になるため施工性が高く、専用マシンの能力を踏まえると、大面積ほど効率が良くなります。大面積で発生しやすいコンクリートのクラックに対しても、高い伸張性を生かし、破断せずに追従します。

It can be used regardless of the area size. It has excellent workability since the material cures and becomes walkable very quickly after spraying. Taking the performance of the special machine into account, the larger the area, the better the efficiency. High extensibility will allow the material to follow without fracturing even on concrete cracks often seen in large area works.

Q どんな下地でも大丈夫？
Can it be used with any kind of foundation?

A （ほぼ）なんでもOK！
(Almost) anything is fine!

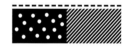

コンクリートはもちろん、ほとんどの金属、プラスティックなどにも接着性が高く、浮き、剥がれがなく、一体の防水膜を形成できます。ジョイント部を含む金属屋根なども得意です。異なる素材の接合でも、その上に一体の防水膜を形成できるので、改修にも向いています。

It is highly adhesive to not only concrete but also most of metals and plastics and can form a uniform waterproofing membrane with no flaking or loose adhesion. It is suitable for metal roofs including joint parts as well. It can also be used for repair of joining of different materials as it can form a uniform membrane on top.

Q 施工やディテールで気をつけることは？
What are the precautions in working and for details?

A 風や紫外線には注意！
Be careful of wind and UV rays!

接着性が高く、端の剥がれがないので、押え金物や笠木は不要。立上りのアゴもいりません。部材の端まで膜を形成して終われます。仕上げの質感については、マットな仕上げが課題です。硬化時間は短いのですが、吹き付けるため、施工時の風には要注意。紫外線が敵！

Neither flashing nor coping are needed with the high adhesive strength. Corbels will not be required as well. It can cover the edges of each part. It needs more improvement to enable matte finishes. While the curing time is short, be careful of wind when working as the material is spread by spraying. UV rays are the enemy!

超速硬化ウレタン複合防水の
ディテールポイント

Detail Points on the Multi-component Ultra Fast Curing Polyurethane Waterproofing Membrane Systems

今回収録した建物を例に、施工上、納まり上の
共通のポイントを押さえておこう。

Let's go over common points in work execution and details,
using the building from this article as an example.

パラペット, 屋根
Parapet, Rooftop

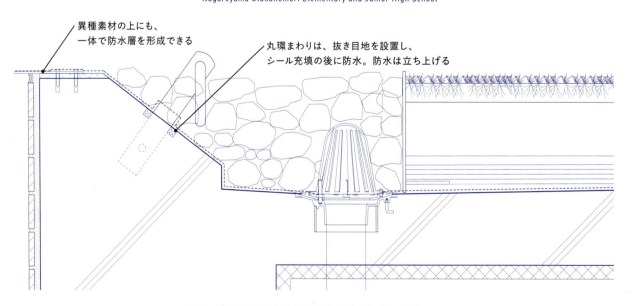

1/8　流山市立おおたかの森小・中学校（→P87）
Nagareyama Otakanomori Elementary and Junior High School

1/8　追手門学院大学120周年記念プロジェクト（→P21）
Otemon Gakuin University 120th Anniversary Project

バルコニー, ウッドデッキ
Balcony, Wooden deck

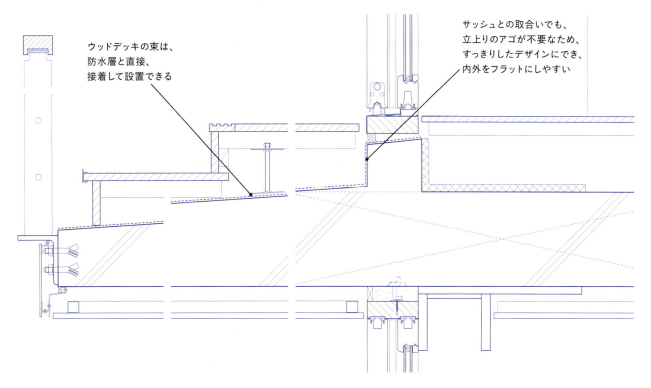

1/10　大阪木材仲買会館（→P91）
Osaka Timber Association Building

庇
Eaves

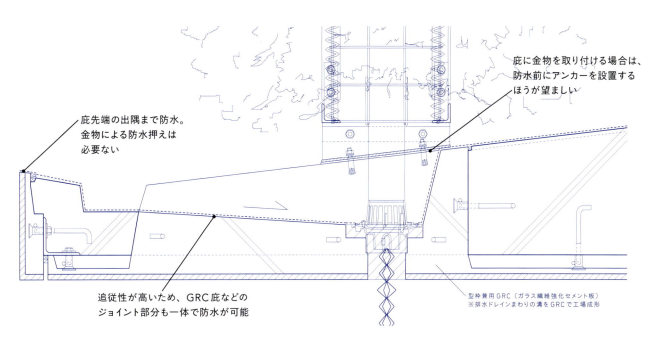

1/10　関西外国語大学 インターナショナルコミュニケーションセンター（→P95）
International Communication Center　Kansai Gaidai University

屋上緑化
Greening

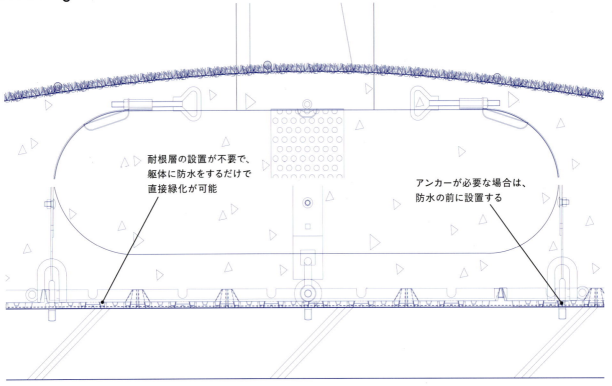

耐根層の設置が不要で、躯体に防水をするだけで直接緑化が可能

アンカーが必要な場合は、防水の前に設置する

1/8　追手門学院大学120周年記念プロジェクト（→P21）
Otemon Gakuin University 120th Anniversary Project

屋上基礎
Rooftop foundation

出隅は5mm以上の面取りをする

アンカーの周囲に抜き目地を設置し、シールを充填した後に防水。防水は立ち上げる

入隅は直角とする

1/5　流山市立おおたかの森小・中学校（→P84）
Nagareyama Otakanomori Elementary and Junior High School

Roof I (P18-37)

Roof II (P38-55)

Curved Roof (P56-71)

Roof + Cladding (P72-83)

Balcony (P84-91)

Eaves (P92-103)

Project (P104-110)

Roof I ── 1

雨水を溜めず，溢れさせる屋根ディテール

Roof Detail Allowing Rainwater Runoff without Collecting It

**追手門学院大学
120周年記念プロジェクト**
三菱地所設計

Otemon Gakuin University
120th Anniversary Project
MITSUBISHI JISHO SEKKEI INC.

施工：大林組・大林道路
構造：1号館／RC造一部S造，6号館／RC造＋梁PC造，
中央棟／S造，守衛所／RC造
規模：1号館／地上3階，地下1階，
6号館＋中央棟／地上11階，地下1階，
守衛所／地上1階
竣工：1号館／2009年8月，
6号館＋中央棟／2006年12月，
守衛所／2006年10月
所在：大阪府茨木市
撮影：黒住直臣

Constructor: OBAYASHI CORPORATION,
OBAYASHI ROAD CORPORATION
Structure: 1st Building／RC+S,
6th Building／RC+PC Beams,
Center Building／S,
Main Gate Building／RC
Number of stories: 1st Building／3 stories,
1 basement,
6th Building+Center Building／11 stories,
1 basement,
Main Gate Building／1 story
Completion date: 1st Building／August, 2009,
6th Building+Center Building／December, 2006,
Main Gate Building／October, 2006
Location: Ibaraki-city, Osaka
Photo: Naoomi Kurozumi

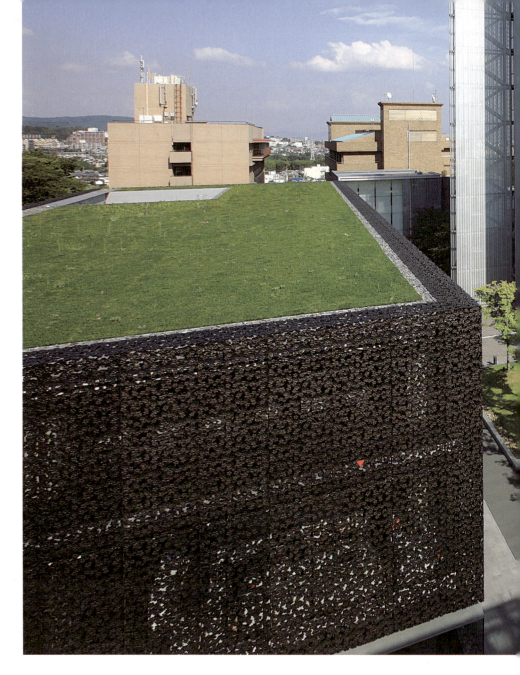

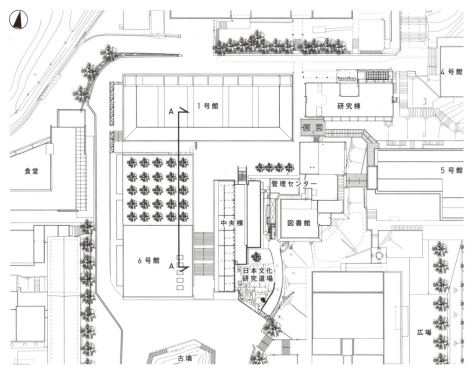

配置（SITE PLAN） 1／1,500

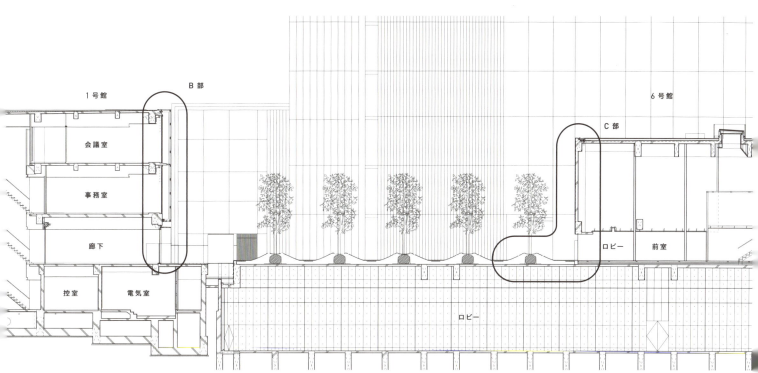

A-A断面（SECTION A-A） 1／300

DETAIL extra issue　19

「桜咲くオフィス」1号館｜アルミキャストの外装と屋上緑化
Offices Amid Cherry Blossoms : 1st Building｜Waterproofing for Cast Aluminum Cladding and Green Roofs

満開の桜の中は賑わいでいっぱいである。1年を通して追手門学院の校章である満開の桜で包むオフィスをつくりたいと考えた。限られた工事費の中で空調負荷を、またガラス性能を抑えるために一番有効なものは、サッシュの外に付く庇やルーバーである。熱負荷を下げる簾のような「満開の桜」を、熱を吸収しやすいアルミでつくり、内外からも桜模様が楽しめるオフィスとした。
防水は先に竣工した6号館で考えた納まりとし、キャストパネルを支持するフラットバーを躯体に直接アンカーし、躯体と鉄部を一体に超速硬化ウレタン複合防水で止水する方法を採用した。アルミキャストパネルと6号館屋上の緑化がシームレスになるディテールである。（三菱地所設計　須部恭浩）

The inner space of full-blooming cherry tree is filled with activity. We felt we wanted to create offices enveloped throughout the year by cherry blossoms—a motif of the Otemon Gakuin badge. The most effective means of reducing the air conditioning load, on a limited budget with reduced glass performance, was to attach eaves and louvers outside the window sashes. Using aluminum, which absorbs heat well, we endeavored to produce a facade of "full-blooming cherries" that would reduce the heat load in the manner of bamboo screens and realize offices that enjoyed cherry flower patterns from both interior and exterior.
For the waterproofing, we chose the same assembly as in 6th Building. After anchoring the flat support bars for the cast aluminum pannel's facade directly to the building frame, we chose a multi-component ultra fast curing polyurethane waterproofing membrane system over the entire building frame and metal attachments. This detail enabled a seamless appearance for the cast aluminum and green roof of 6th building.
(MITSUBISHI JISHO SEKKEI INC.　Yasuhiro Sube)

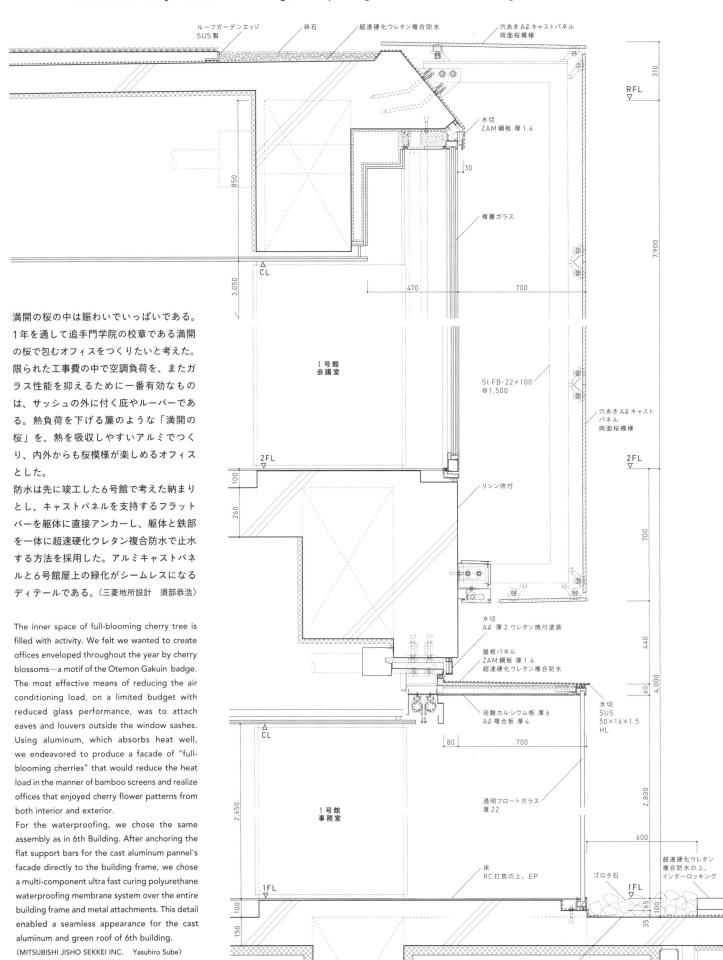

B部断面詳細（DETAILED SECTION B）　1／20

6号館 | 地面と一体に見せる屋上緑化
6th Building | Green Roofs Visually Unified with the Ground

コンペの要求にて巨大な建物を山の上に計画することになった。既にあった建物の眺望を遮ることないよう、三つの中教室と大教室で構成する6号館を低層化することにした。三つの中教室は斜面地を生かして地中に埋没し、建物の屋根面を広場として緑化し高木のケヤキを配置した。また、大教室は食堂から望む視線を確保できる高さで地上部に設置し、屋上をタマリュウシート張りで緑化した。（三菱地所設計　須部恭浩）

In answer to the conditions of the design competition, we designed a "large building on a mountain." To avoid blocking views from existing buildings, we composed 6th Building as a low volume containing three intermediate-size and one large-size classroom. Taking advantage of the slope, we placed the three intermediate-size classrooms underground and greenified their roof to create a plaza planted with tall zelkova trees. We then placed the large classroom above ground at a height within view of the cafeteria and greenified its roof with sheets of mondo grass. (MITSUBISHI JISHO SEKKEI INC.　Yasuhiro Sube)

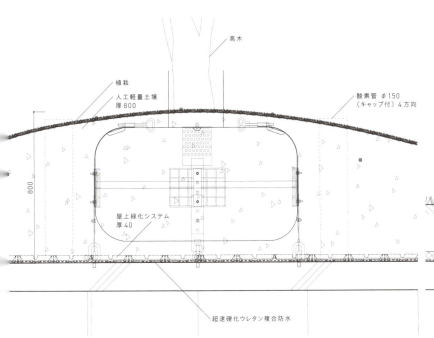

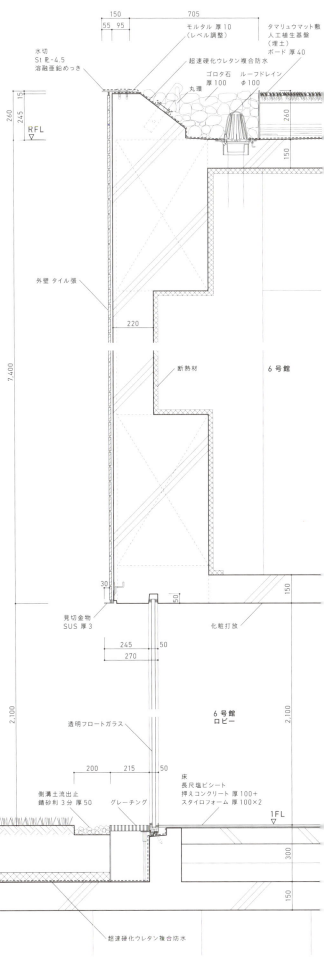

C部断面詳細 (DETAILED SECTION C) 1/20

中央棟｜ダブルスキンの頂部ディテール
Center Building｜Detailing at the Top of a Double-skin Facade

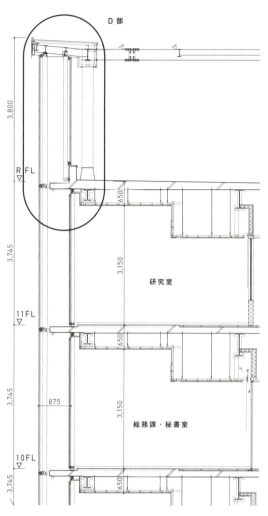

矩計（SECTION） 1／100

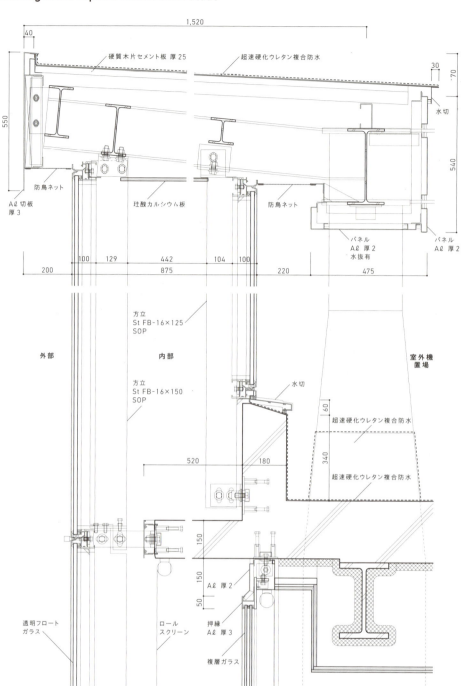

D部断面詳細（DETAILED SECTION D） 1／15

眺望を最大限確保し、研究室内でも授業をできるようにとのクライアントからの要望で、間口6m、奥行き5mの30㎡の研究室を積層している。敷地の条件から東西面に開口を設けるため、ダブルスキンとして熱環境の向上を図った上で、床から天井まで大開口のガラスとした。層間区画およびキャビティ内の清掃を踏まえた500mmのPCスラブは高所で足元が怖くならない効果もある。コストを踏まえサッシ枠を同一形状にし、全層換気とした。ダブルスキン西側は、屋上機械の目隠しのためキャビティガラスを屋上レベルより1層立ち上げ、東側はダブルスキンサッシとパラペットがない笠木部の取合いとした。（三菱地所設計　須部恭浩）

The client desired to be able to hold classes in the laboratory rooms. In response, we stacked laboratory rooms 30㎡ in size with a 6m frontage and 5m depth while maintaining exterior views to the maximum degree. In order to establish windows on the east and west sides, as demanded by site conditions, we used a double skin to improve the thermal environment and installed large floor-to-ceiling windows. A precast-concrete slab 500mm in depth, established inside the double-skin cavity as a fire barrier between floors and for cleaning the cavity, alleviates any fear arising from looking down through floor-to-ceiling windows on the higher floors. For cost savings, window sashes on all floors have the same shape, and the double skin is designed for air circulation between floors. On the west side, the double skin rises higher than the roof to hide the rooftop equipment, while on the east side, a coping assembly with no double-skin sash or parapet is employed. (MITSUBISHI JISHO SEKKEI INC. Yasuhiro Sube)

守衛所｜ドレーンを設けず雨を落とすディテール
Main Gate Building｜Detailing for Shedding Rainwater Without a Drain

大学の正門には守衛所があることが多い。正門と守衛所を分けてつくるのが一般的だが、これらを一体化し、建築を象徴的な正門にできないかと考えた。横長とすることで、後部部に広がる駐車場の管理門扉と一体化でき、将来守衛所が無人化になった際にはタクシーやバスなどの待合として改修できるように、躯体をあらかじめコの字形にして将来の正門のあり方を予測した形状とした。ケヤキや桜並木が周辺にあり飛来する落ち葉がドレーンに詰まることがあるため、ドレーンを設けず、雨水を落とす計画とし、メンテナンスに配慮した。（三菱地所設計　須部恭浩）

Many university gates have a guard room. Usually, the gate and guardroom are separate facilities, but we wanted to unify them in a gate having symbolic architectural character. By creating a long volume, we could integrate the gate with the administrative gate of the parking area to the rear. Furthermore, anticipating future needs, we shaped its structural frame in a horizontal U. The gate thus possesses a built-in capability for renovation as a waiting room for taxis and buses should the conventional guard-man be replaced by automation. Because leaves falling from the row of zelkova and cherry trees might clog a drain, we created a thin design without a drain for ease of maintenance.
（MITSUBISHI JISHO SEKKEI INC.　Yasuhiro Sube）

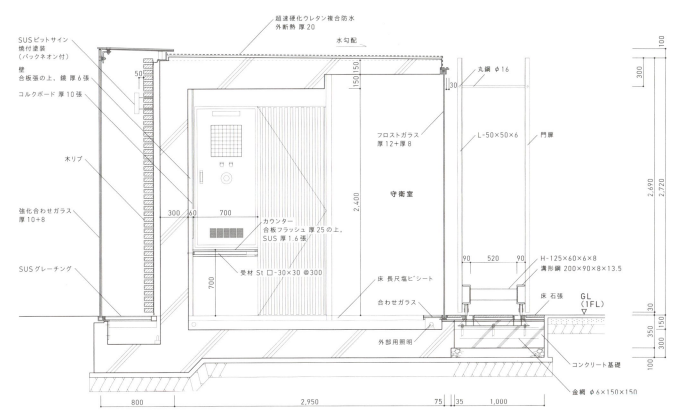

断面詳細（DETAILED SECTION）　1／40

Roof I

2

コンクリートパネルで2重スラブをつくる

Creating Double Slabs with Concrete Panels

豊中市立文化芸術センター
日建設計

Toyonaka Performing Arts Center
NIKKEN SEKKEI LTD

施工：大林組・河崎組特定建設工事共同企業体
構造：RM造，一部RC造・SRC造・S造
規模：地上3階，地下1階，塔屋1階
竣工：2016年8月
所在：大阪府豊中市
撮影：東出写真事務所（p24, 26），木原慎二（p27）

Constructor: OBAYASHI, KAWASAKIGUMI JV
Structure: RM+RC+SRC+S
Number of stories: 3 stories, 1 basement,
1 Rooftop structure
Completion date: August, 2016
Location: Toyonaka-city, Osaka
Photo: Higashide photo studio (p24, 26),
Shinji Kihara (p27)

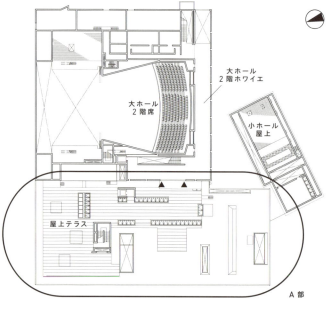

3階平面（3rd FLOOR PLAN） 1／1,200

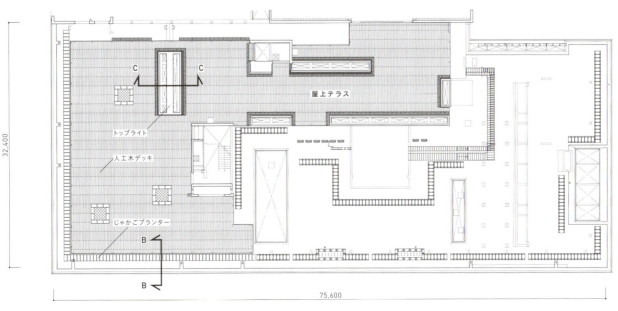

A部平面（PLAN A） 1／500

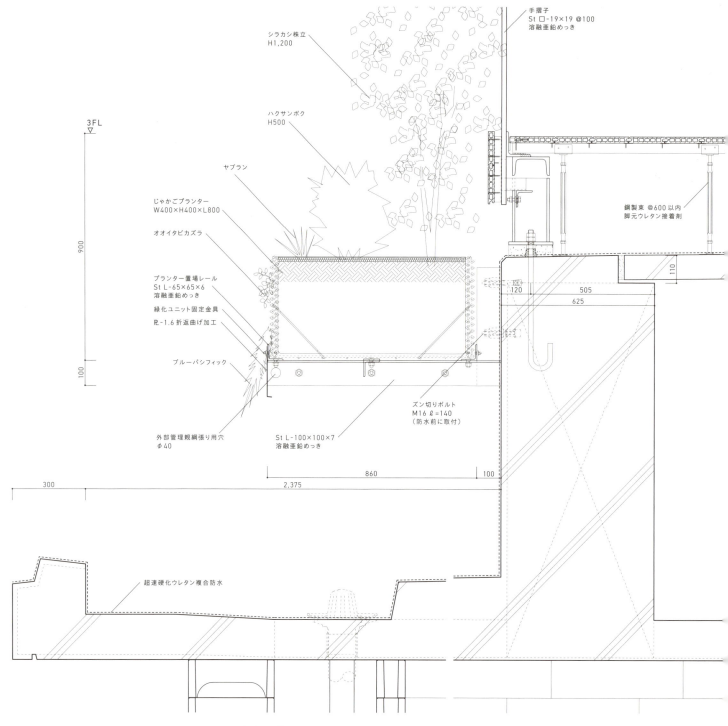

D・E部断面詳細（DETAILED SECTION D,E） 1／15

大・小ホールを中心とした文化創造拠点として、建物全体がギャラリー空間であるこの建築は、使う素材を厳選し「床」は無垢材のフローリング、「壁」は鉄筋コンクリート組積造（RM造）、「天井」はRC打放しとすることで非日常の風景を演出。
美しいRC打放し天井を実現するために、照明やスプリンクラーなどの設備を計画的に納める2重スラブを採用し、室内側に打放しRCスラブ、設備配管等の施工後、上部にコンクリートパネルを敷き並べ超速硬化ウレタン複合防水を吹き付ける。この防水の特徴として、異種取合いを含め基本的に動かないものであれば、すべてを防水で覆うことが可能で、防水の仕舞の端部を金物等で押さえる必要がなく場所を選ばない。ウレタン防水の上は、直接歩行することも可能であるが、人工木材のデッキ、緑化ブロックなどで仕上げることで、市民に開放された屋上庭園を実現している。（日建設計　多喜茂）

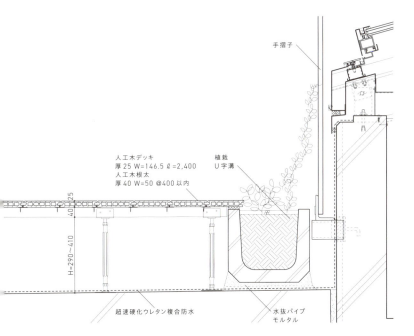

The building is a culture creation base that centers around its main and lesser halls, with the whole structure functioning as a gallery space. With natural wood flooring for the "floor", reinforced concrete masonry (RM) for the "walls" and exposed RC for the "ceiling", the carefully selected materials create a unique ambience.
To achieve a beautiful exposed RC ceiling, double slabs have been used in order to systematically house fittings such as lighting and sprinklers, etc., with the exposed RC slabs on the interior side and, after the installation of utility piping, etc., concrete panels laid on the upper side and sprayed with multi-component ultra fast curing polyurethane waterproofing membrane systems. The special features of this waterproofing are that, as long as there is no movement, mixed material surfaces can be completely coated, and in any location, without the need to cap the ends of the waterproofing finish with metal fixtures, etc. It is possible to walk on top of the urethane waterproofing, but by finishing it off with artificial wood decking and green blocks, etc., a rooftop garden space has been created that can be enjoyed by the public. (NIKKEN SEKKEI LTD Shigeru Taki)

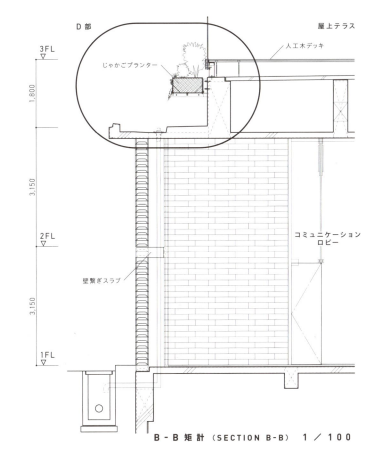

B-B 矩計 (SECTION B-B)　1／100

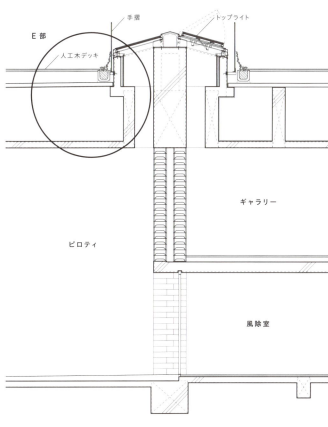

C-C 矩計 (SECTION C-C)　1／100

Roof I — 3

オープンスペースが
主役の，
丘を生かした
低層の庁舎

Emphasizing an Open Space
with a Low Volume Giving Play
to Surrounding Hills

長崎県庁舎
日建設計，松林建築設計事務所，池田設計

Nagasaki Prefecture Office
NIKKEN SEKKEI LTD,
MATSUBAYASHI ARCHITECTURAL DESIGN OFFICE,
IKEDA ARCHITECTS

施工：行政棟／鹿島・上滝・堀内特定建設工事共同企業体，
議会棟／堀内・小山・松崎特定建設工事共同企業体
構造：RC造，一部木造
規模：地上8階
竣工：2017年11月
所在：長崎県長崎市
撮影：雁光舎 野田東徳（p28下，30，31），
株式会社エスエス 上田新一郎（p33）
写真提供：ダイフレックス（p28上）

Constructor: Administrative Building／KAJIMA,
JOTAKI, HORIUCHI JV, Assembly Building／
HORIUCHI, KOYAMA, MATSUZAKI JV
Structure: RC+W
Number of stories: 8 stories
Completion date: November, 2017
Location: Nagasaki-city, Nagasaki
Photo: Gankosha Harunori Noda（p28lower, 30,
31）, SS Co., Ltd. Shinichiro Ueda（p33）
Courtesy of: Dyflex Co., Ltd.（p28upper）

28　DETAIL extra issue

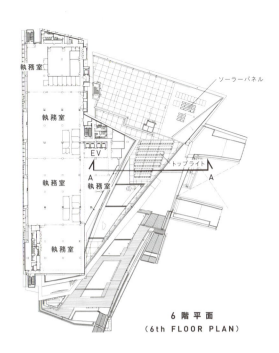

6階平面
(6th FLOOR PLAN)

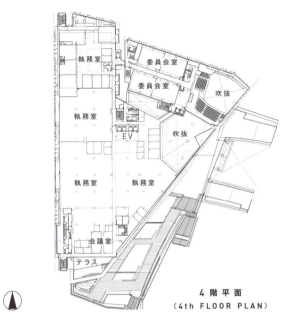

4階平面
(4th FLOOR PLAN)

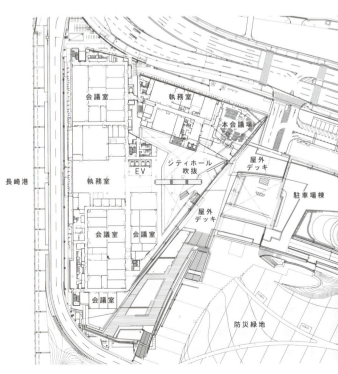

3階平面 (3rd FLOOR PLAN)
1／1,500

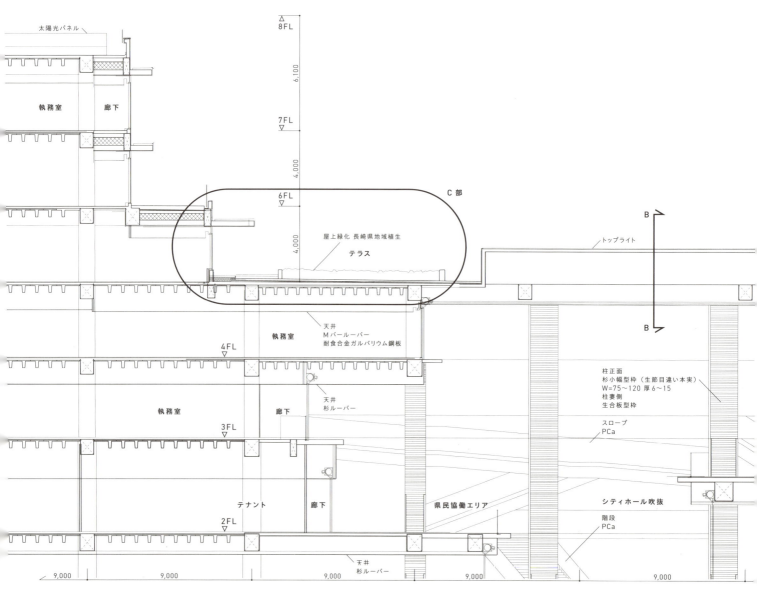

A-A断面（SECTION A-A） 1／200

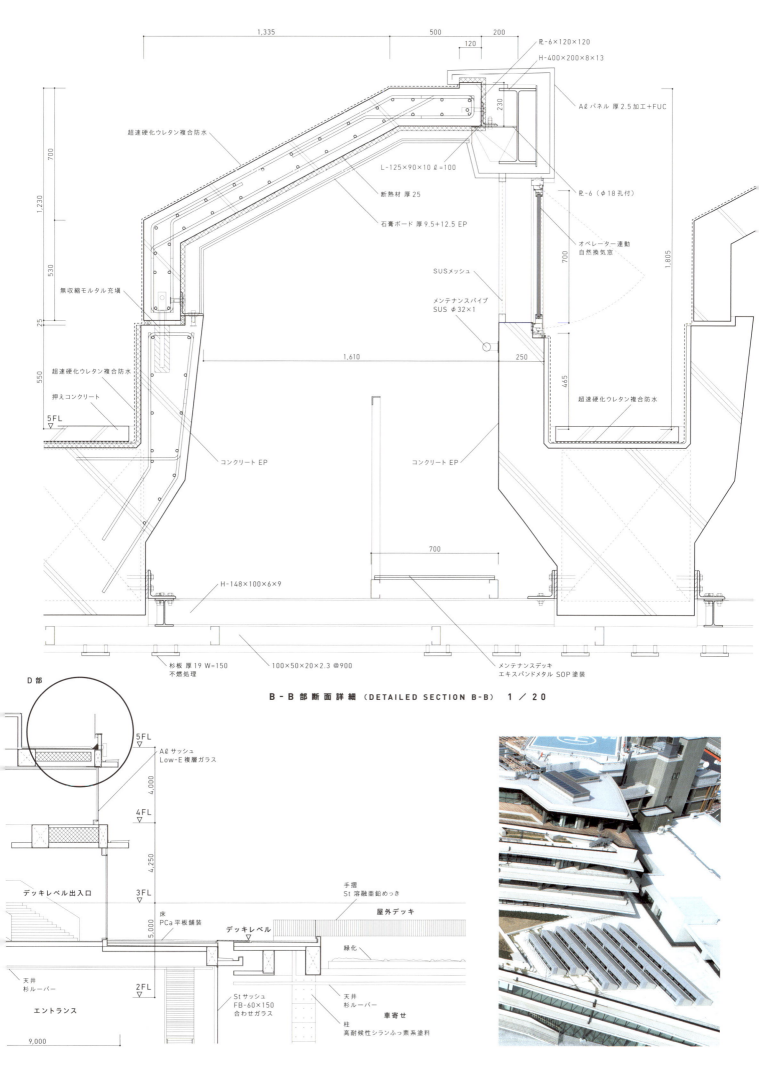

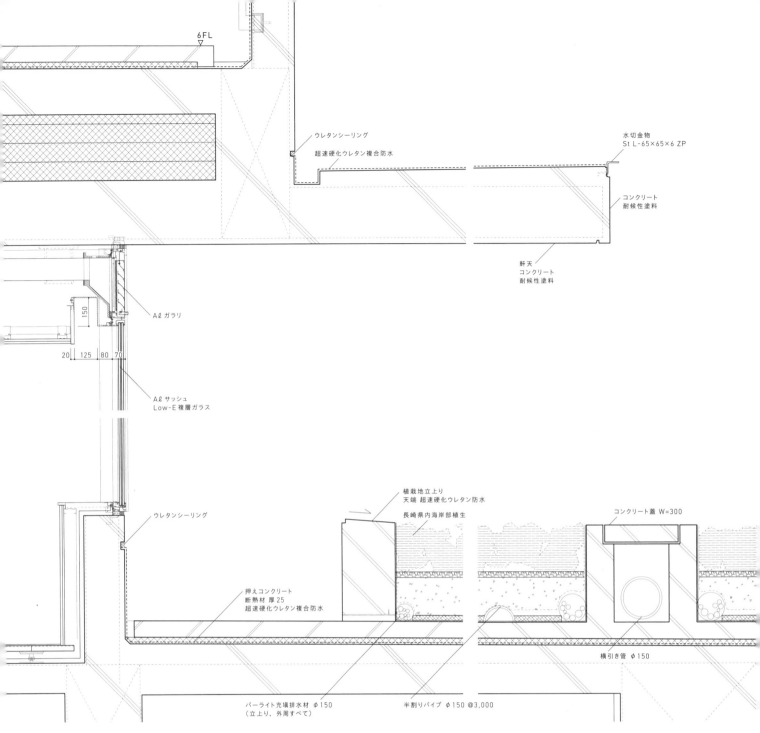

C 部断面詳細 (DETAILED SECTION C) 1 / 20

基本構想で示された18階建ての高層庁舎は、丘に囲まれた長崎の景観には高すぎると感じ、震災後の経験から低層に抑えた庁舎が拠点にはふさわしいと考え、テラス状に8階の各層をセットバックさせた庁舎を提案した。庁舎の各階のテラスから足元に広がる海辺のオープンスペースは、隣接する防災緑地、駐車場棟、警察本部庁舎と連なり、平地が少ない長崎で人々に屋外活動の場を提供するとともに、非常時の災害救援活動の場を提供することもできる。

オープンスペースや各庁舎棟とつながる2～3階の屋上デッキは、一体的に同じ仕様で施工可能な超速硬化ウレタン複合防水を用いることで、屋上緑化や床仕上の異なる部分の相互の境界を曖昧にすることができ、それにより空間がシェアされ、県民の交流が生まれ、創発を生むのではなかろうかと考えている。結果として、庁舎全体は一続きの丘のような様相を呈することになったが、「丘のような庁舎」をつくることを意図したわけではなく、むしろ、庁舎から強いジオメトリーを消し去り、オープンスペースを主役にして、長崎の景観を生み出している「丘を生かす」庁舎をつくることこそが目指すところであった。(日建設計　山梨知彦・高橋央・平井友介)

The 18-floor high-rise government building shown in the basic concept was too tall, we felt, for the scenic hills encompassing Nagasaki. From past disaster experience, as well, we believed a low-rise building would best suit a disaster management headquarters. We therefore proposed a building of eight setback floors arranged in a terraced format. An open space unfolds from the terrace of each floor to the seaside areas below, across the adjacent disaster prevention green space, parking building, and police headquarters building. The open space offers places for activities to people in Nagasaki, a city with few flat areas, and a place for disaster relief efforts in times of emergency.

A multi-component ultra fast curing polyurethane waterproofing membrane system, applicable using uniform specifications over an entire area, was employed in the open spaces of the rooftops and second and third floor decks. By this means, we could soften the boundaries between the areas of green roof and flooring, with result that spaces are shared, interchange is born among prefectural residents, and a synergy of activity arises. The completed government building appears somewhat like a ranging hill, but creating a "hill-like government building" was not our intention. To the contrary, our aim was to erase strong geometry from the government building and reinforce the presence of the open space, thereby creating a government building that "gives play to the hills" of Nagasaki's scenic surroundings. (NIKKEN SEKKEI LTD Tomohiko Yamanashi, Hiroshi Takahashi, Yusuke Hirai)

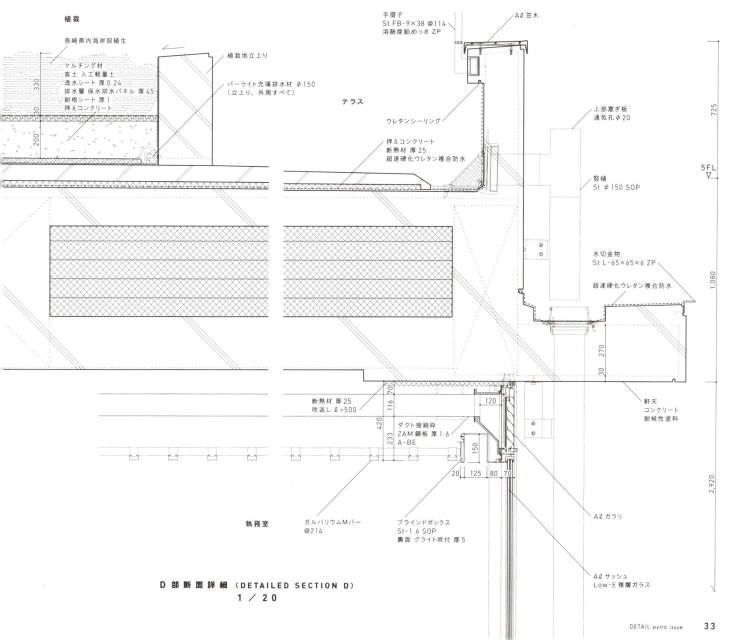

D部断面詳細（DETAILED SECTION D）
1／20

Roof I — 4

都市に立体的な
アクティビティを
発現させる

Manifesting Activity
Three-dimensionally in the City

立川市立第一小学校，柴崎図書館
小嶋一浩＋赤松佳珠子／CAt

Tachikawa Daiichi Elementary School,
Shibasaki Library
Kazuhiro Kojima + Kazuko Akamatsu / CAt

施工：大成建設
構造：RC造，一部S造・SRC造
規模：地上3階，地下1階
竣工：2014年8月
所在：東京都立川市
撮影：西川公朗

Constructor: TAISEI CORPORATION
Structure: RC+S+SRC
Number of stories: 3 stories, 1 basement
Completion date: August, 2014
Location: Tachikawa-city, Tokyo
Photo: Masao Nishikawa

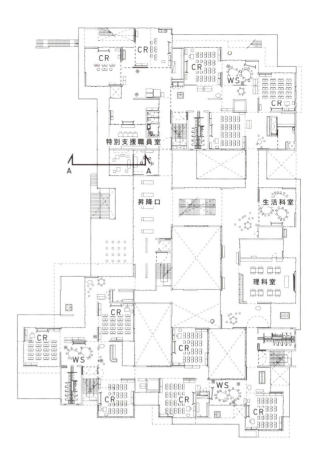

2階平面 (2nd FLOOR PLAN) 1／800

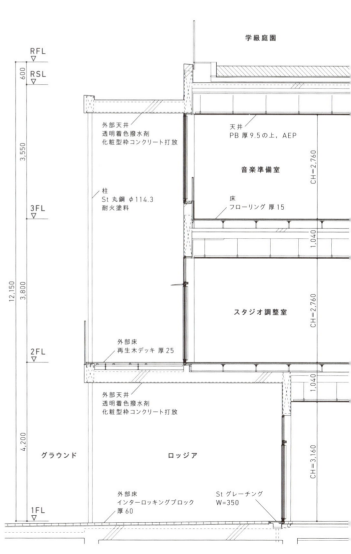

A－A矩計 (SECTION A-A) 1／100

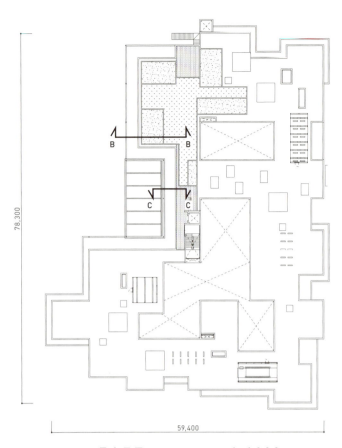

屋上平面（ROOF PLAN） 1／800

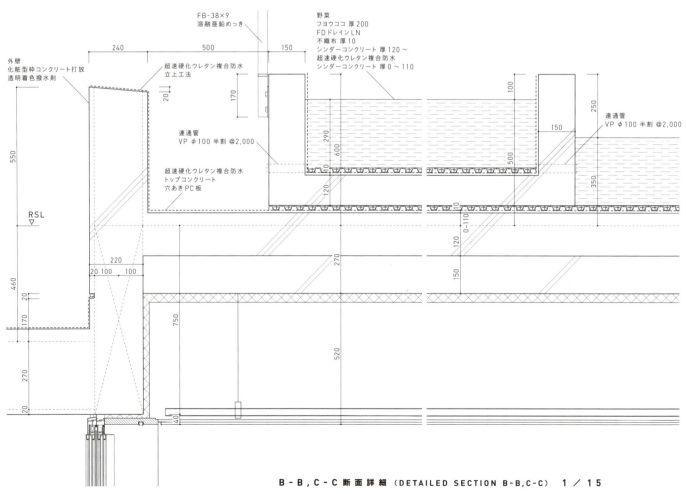

B-B，C-C断面詳細（DETAILED SECTION B-B,C-C） 1／15

立川市立第一小学校は、立川市で最も長い歴史のある学校で、平成21年度には学校創立140周年の記念行事が行われている。しかし、築50年を経過し、耐震性の問題があるため、新しい校舎に建て替えることになった。建替えにあたって、柴崎学習館と、本来小学校に隣接されるべき柴崎学童保育所を一体の施設として複合化させることになり、児童の安全と良好な教育環境を備えた学校施設、地域の核となる防災拠点としての機能をあわせもつ施設となることを目指した。

敷地がそれほど大きくないなか、子供たちの活動域としてのデッキスペース、屋上庭園などを、採光を確保しつつ最大限確保し、立体的にアクティビティが展開する場をつくることを目指した。各階にあるアクティビティのきっかけとなる手洗い場、屋上庭園、水田、さまざまな形状のベンチに加え、手摺などもあり、取合いの種類が増えることは設計上苦心した点であった。

そういった建築の特性に対し、超速硬化ウレタン複合防水は床懐が小さい部分、複雑な形状に対しても施工性がよいなど、ディテールの自由度が高いことが、多様な場をつくることを目指した設計の考えと合致し、その実現に貢献している。（CAt 和泉有祐）

Tachikawa Daiichi Elementary School, Tachikawa's historically oldest school, observed its 140th anniversary in fiscal 2009. The fifty-year-old school building lacked sufficient seismic resistance, however, so a decision was made to construct a new building. The new design would combine the school with the public hall and an after-school day-care center to create a building complex, with the aim of realizing a school facility with a good educational environment, well equipped for child safety and as a disaster prevention center for the region.

The site was not large. In these circumstances, we endeavored to provide a deck space, roof garden, and other spaces for children's activities, while securing sufficient daylighting, so as to create a place where activities can unfold in three dimensions. Along with the elements promoting activities on each floor—the wash place, roof garden, rice field, and benches of all shapes—there are also handrails, and integrating an increasing variety of things became the aspect of design demanding the greatest attention.

In response to the special character of the architecture, as such, the freedom offered by a multi-component ultra fast curing polyurethane waterproofing membrane system—particularly its ease of use on complex shapes and in small spaces under the flooring—suited the spatial diversity of the design and contributed to its realization. （CAt Yusuke Izumi）

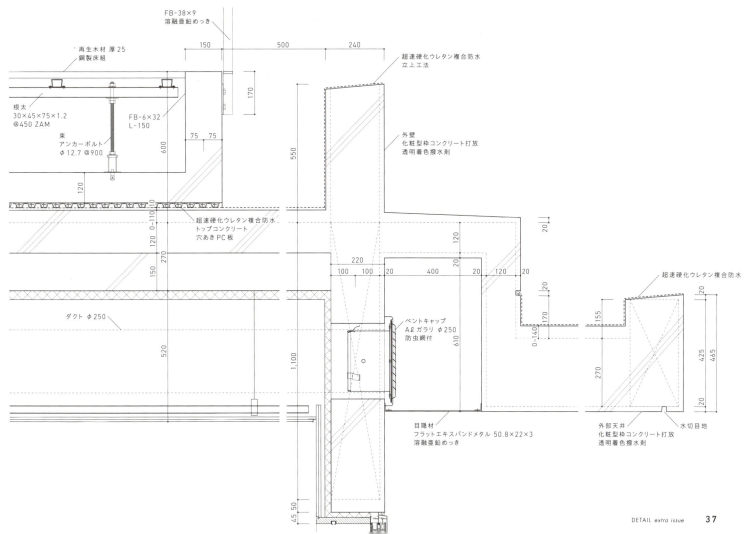

Roof II — 5

屋内と
シームレスに
つながる
屋上テラス

Connecting a Rooftop Terrace
Seamlessly with Interior Spaces

愛知県立愛知総合工科高等学校
久米設計

Aichi High School of Technology and Engineering
KUME SEKKEI Co., Ltd.

施工：戸田・名工特定建設工事共同企業体
構造：RC造，一部S造
規模：地上5階
竣工：2016年3月
所在：愛知県名古屋市
撮影：林広明（p38, 41）
写真提供：久米設計（p40）

Constructor: Toda, Meiko JV
Structure: RC+S
Number of stories: 5 stories
Completion date: March, 2016
Location: Nagoya-city, Aichi
Photo: Hiroaki Hayashi (p38, 41)
Courtesy of: KUME SEKKEI Co., Ltd. (p40)

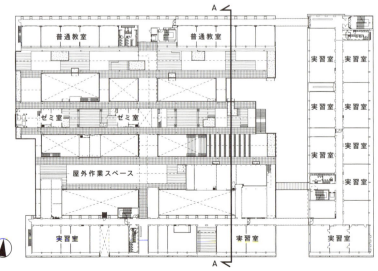

3階平面 (3rd FLOOR PLAN) 1／1,500

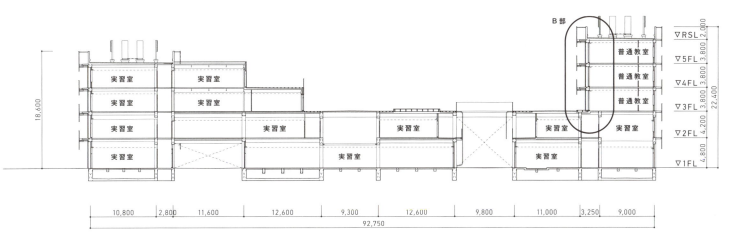

A－A断面（SECTION A-A） 1／600

実習室が校舎全体の約7割を占める、ものづくりの学校である。低層部の屋根を屋上テラスとし、実習室間の移動や休憩など生徒の居場所として有効活用した。

この屋上テラスをつくるうえで課題としたことは次の3点である。1点目は生徒の移動を妨げないよう屋内外をシームレスに連続させること、2点目は周辺への圧迫感を軽減するため階高を上げずに防水処理を行うこと、3点目は防水立上りをカバーしフラットに納めるための浮床の使用を抑えることである。

排水勾配を綿密に計画し、幅を広くし高さを抑えた排水帯をストライプ状に配置することでゲリラ豪雨にも対応できる排水能力を確保した。この排水帯部分のみを浮床とすることでコストを抑えつつシームレスに連続する屋上空間を実現した。端部の防水立上りは手摺金物を下地とし浮床とフラットに納めることでスッキリとしたディテールとした。（久米設計　横田順）

C部断面詳細（DETAILED SECTION C）1／8

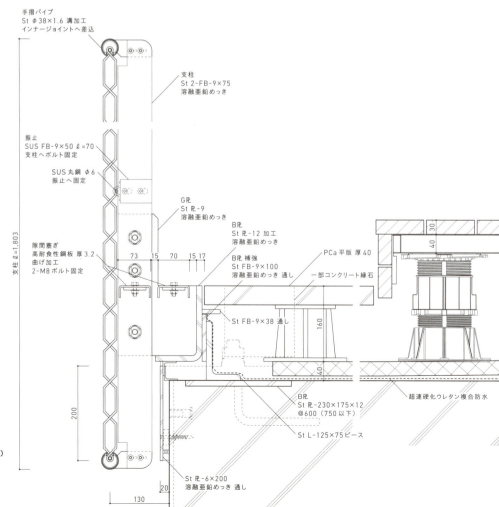

At this school, training rooms occupy about 70% of the entire school building. The roof of the low volume has a rooftop terrace utilized effectively as an area for the students to be, such as when moving between training classes or simply relaxing.
Three issues guided the design of this rooftop terrace. First was seamless continuance of interior and exterior spaces for unhampered movement of students, and second, to install a waterproofing system without raising the floor height. Third was to conceal the containment and use a floating floor to make the deck flat.
By carefully planning the deck's drainage pitch and installing a wide, shallow zone (trough) along each edge, we obtained drainage capability sufficient even for sudden "guerrilla" downpours. By installing a floating floor only in the drainage zones, we furthermore restrained costs and achieved a seamless floor space. The containments at each edge, situated on handrail hardware, are flat and flush with the floating floor, for detailing of sharp and simple appearance. (KUME SEKKEI Co., Ltd. Jun Yokota)

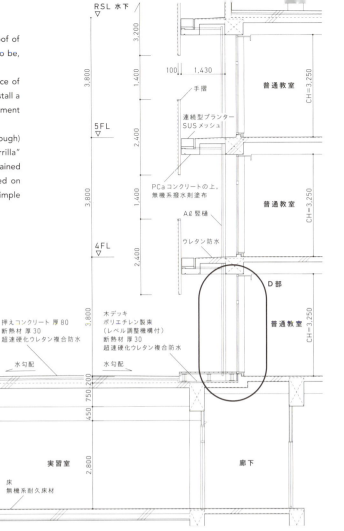

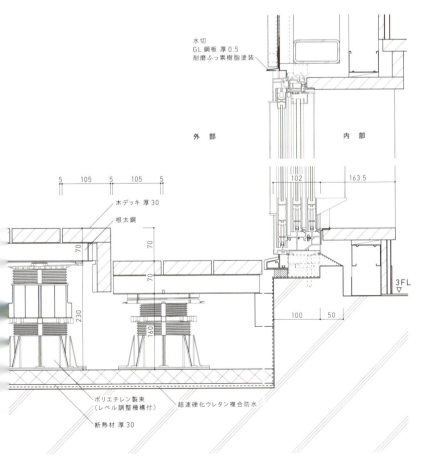

B 部断面 (SECTION B)　1／120

D 部断面詳細 (DETAILED SECTION D)　1／8

Roof II — 6

海外での超高層の屋上防水と緑化防水

Rooftop and Green Roof Waterproofing for a High-rise Building Overseas

臺北南山廣場
三菱地所設計，瀚亞國際設計

Taipei Nanshan Plaza
MITSUBISHI JISHO SEKKEI INC.,
ARCHASIA DESIGN GROUP

施工：互助營造
構造：地上／S造，地下／SRC造＋RC造
規模：地上48階，地下5階，塔屋2階
竣工：2018年1月
所在：台湾台北市
撮影：鈴木久雄（p42，44，45，46左），
新建築社写真部（p46右）

Constructor: Futsu Construction Co., Ltd.
Structure: Ground／S, Underground／SRC+RC
Number of stories: 48 stories, 5 basements,
2 Rooftop structures
Completion date: January, 2018
Location: Taipei-city, Taiwan
Photo: Hisao Suzuki（p42, 44, 45, 46left），
Shinkenchiku-sha（p46right）

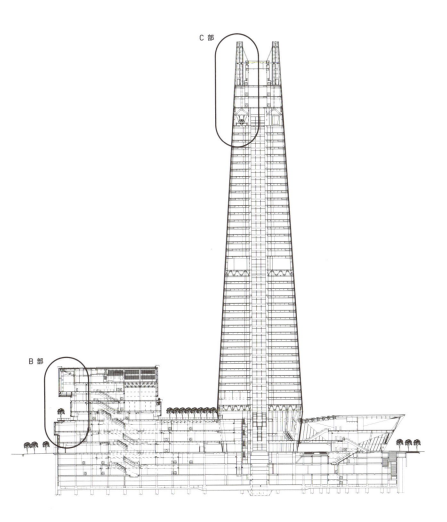

A-A断面 (SECTION A-A) 1／2,500

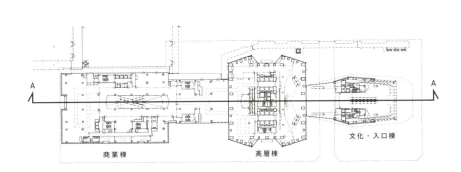

2階平面 (2nd FLOOR PLAN) 1／2,500

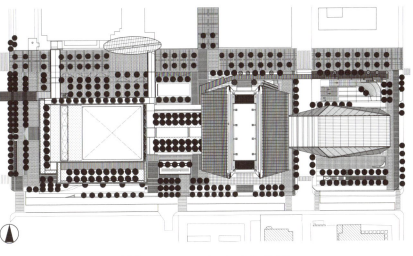

配置 (SITE PLAN) 1／2,500

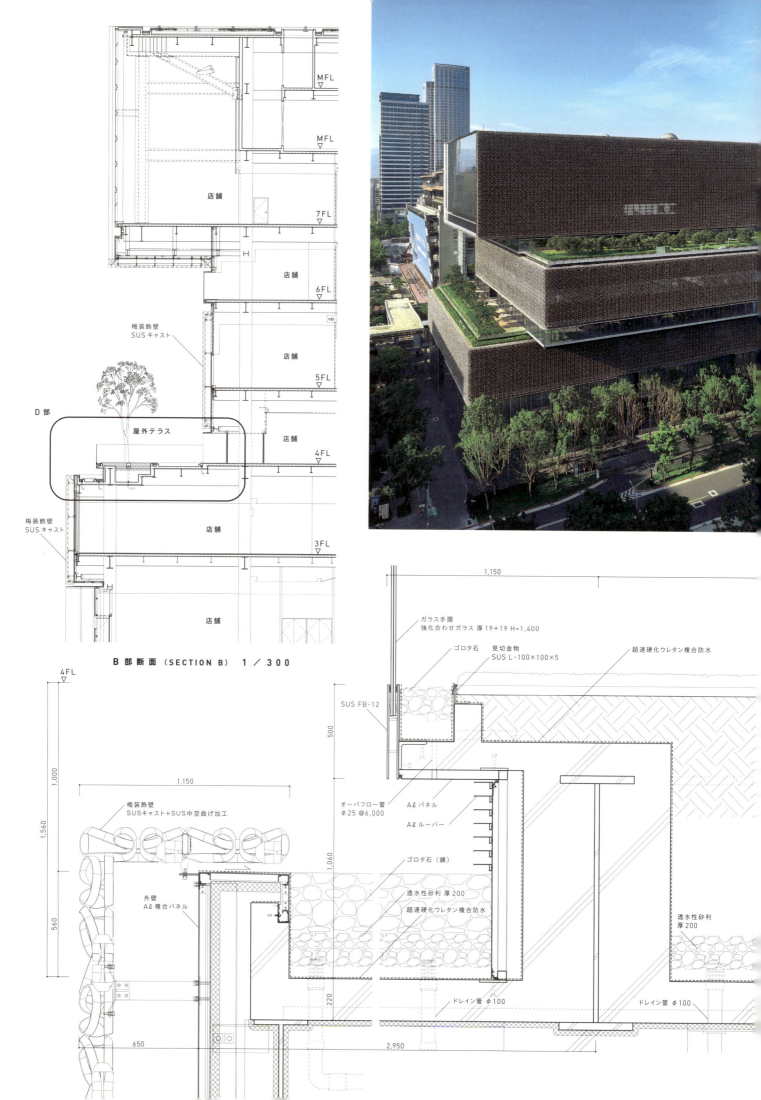

B部断面（SECTION B） 1／300

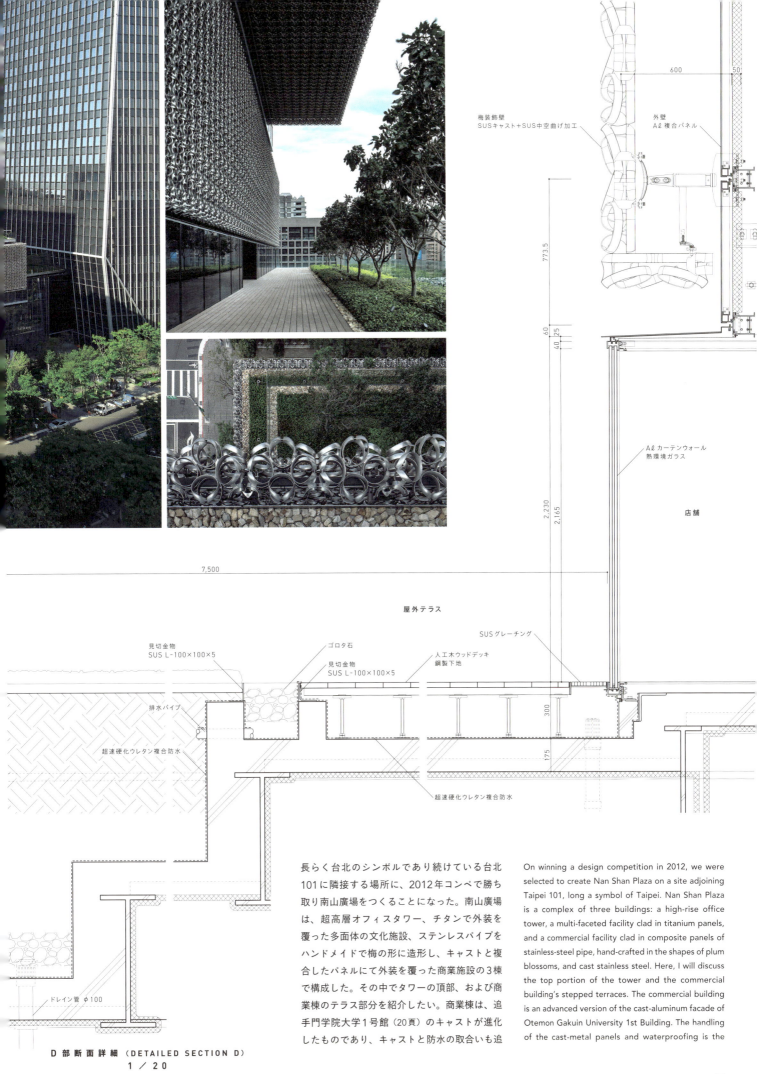

D部断面詳細（DETAILED SECTION D）
1／20

長らく台北のシンボルであり続けている台北101に隣接する場所に、2012年コンペで勝ち取り南山廣場をつくることになった。南山廣場は、超高層オフィスタワー、チタンで外装を覆った多面体の文化施設、ステンレスパイプをハンドメイドで梅の形に造形し、キャストと複合したパネルにて外装を覆った商業施設の3棟で構成した。その中でタワーの頂部、および商業棟のテラス部分を紹介したい。商業棟は、追手門学院大学1号館（20頁）のキャストが進化したものであり、キャストと防水の取合いも追

On winning a design competition in 2012, we were selected to create Nan Shan Plaza on a site adjoining Taipei 101, long a symbol of Taipei. Nan Shan Plaza is a complex of three buildings: a high-rise office tower, a multi-faceted facility clad in titanium panels, and a commercial facility clad in composite panels of stainless-steel pipe, hand-crafted in the shapes of plum blossoms, and cast stainless steel. Here, I will discuss the top portion of the tower and the commercial building's stepped terraces. The commercial building is an advanced version of the cast-aluminum facade of Otemon Gakuin University 1st Building. The handling of the cast-metal panels and waterproofing is the

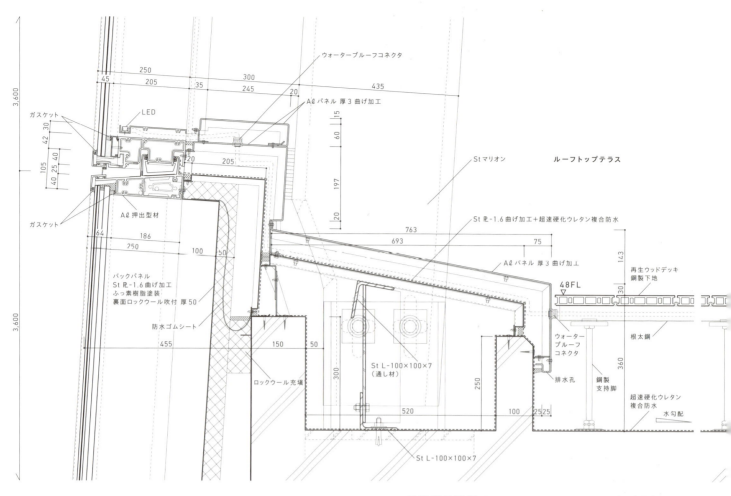

E部断面詳細（DETAILED SECTION E） 1／10

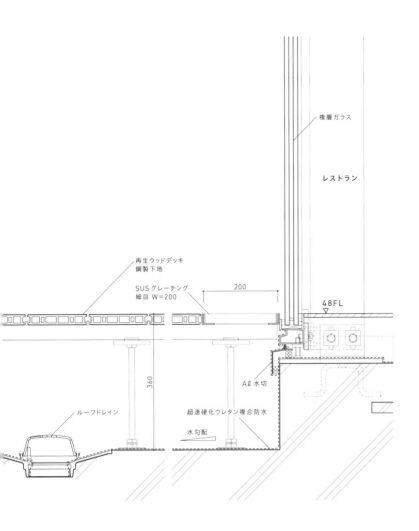

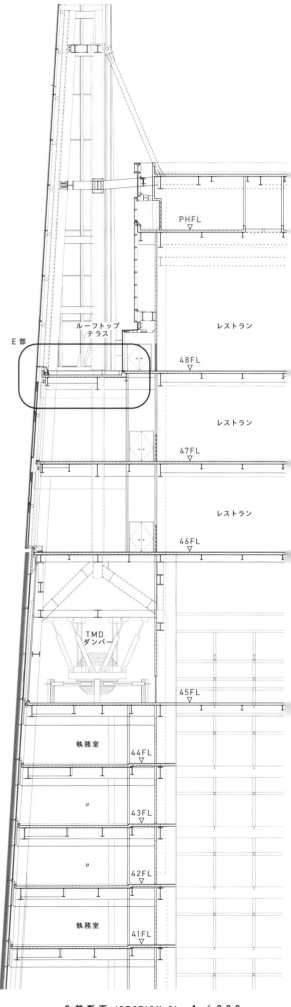

手門学院と同様である。
台湾は地震が多く、台風が頻繁に通る南国の亜熱帯地域である。さらに超高層ビルでの防水であるため、デザイン上またメンテナンス上、シンプルな防水として何がふさわしいか議論し、超速硬化ウレタン複合防水を採用した。近年海外での事例でアスファルト防水を使う機会は減ってきている。アスファルト防水よりウレタン防水の施工が簡易で保証も同等なのが理由と聞く。以前、クライアント指定の標準ディテールの植栽部における防水は、根伸び対策としてアスファルト防水の押えコンクリートの上にステンレス防水をするスペックであったが、施工者の保証を踏まえ、超速硬化ウレタン複合防水のみでも耐えられるという判断となり施工が実現している。(三菱地所設計　須部恭浩)

same as in the design of Otemon Gakuin.
Taiwan is a southern, sub-tropical country that frequently experiences typhoons. It is also prone to earthquakes. Considering these conditions and the special needs of a skyscraper building's roofing, we sought a waterproofing method simple in both design and maintenance, and chose a multi-component ultra fast curing polyurethane waterproofing membrane system. Occasions for using asphalt waterproofing are decreasing in overseas projects recent years. The reason, one hears, is that polyurethane waterproofing is easier to apply than asphalt and equally impermeable. Until now, when waterproofing a vegetation cover, a standard detail was to lay stainless-steel waterproofing over the protective concrete layer, above the asphalt waterproofing, for resistance to root penetration. This time, however, backed by the builder's guarantee, it was determined that a multi-component ultra fast curing polyurethane waterproofing membrane system alone would suffice, and the application of such a membrane system was achieved.
(MITSUBISHI JISHO SEKKEI INC., Yasuhiro Sube)

C部断面 (SECTION C) 1／300

Roof II

7

31m以下に7層の階高を最大限確保するために必要な屋上ディテール

Roof Detailing to Secure Maximum Ceiling Height in 7 Floors at Maximum 31m

W-place
三菱地所設計

W-place
MITSUBISHI JISHO SEKKEI INC.

施工：大成建設
構造：S造
規模：地上7階
竣工：2007年10月
所在：大阪府大阪市
撮影：黒住直臣

Constructor: TAISEI CORPORATION
Structure: S
Number of stories: 7 stories
Completion date: October, 2007
Location: Osaka-city, Osaka
Photo: Naoomi Kurozumi

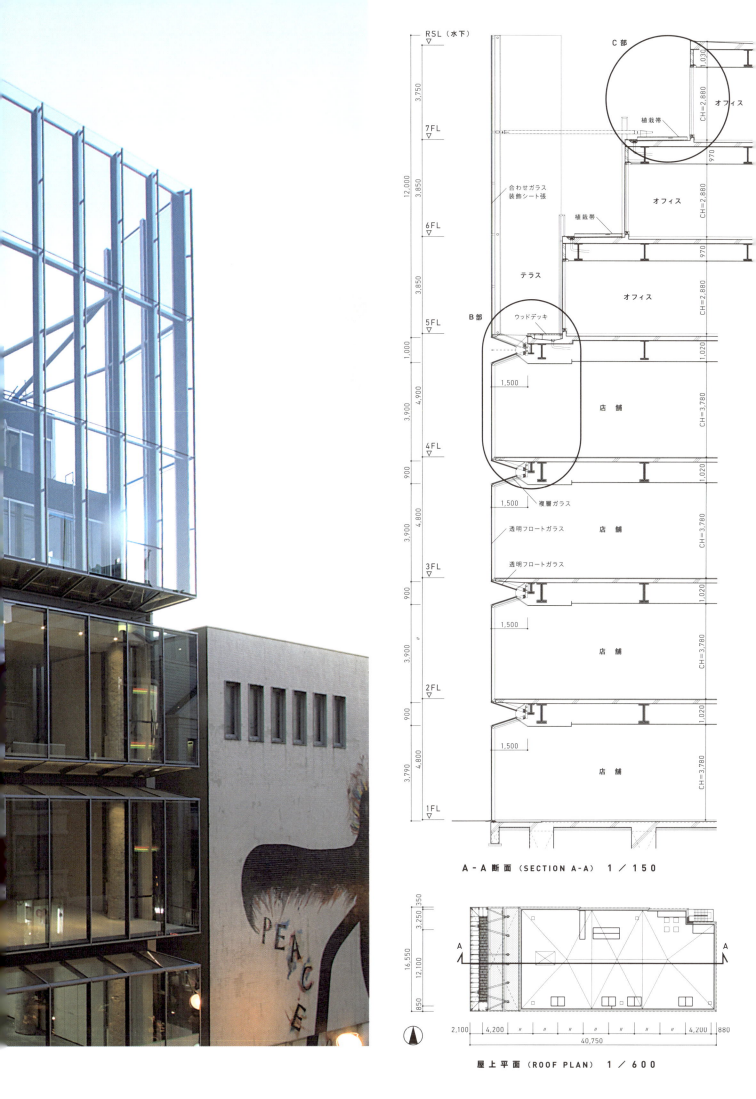

A-A 断面（SECTION A-A） 1／150

屋上平面（ROOF PLAN） 1／600

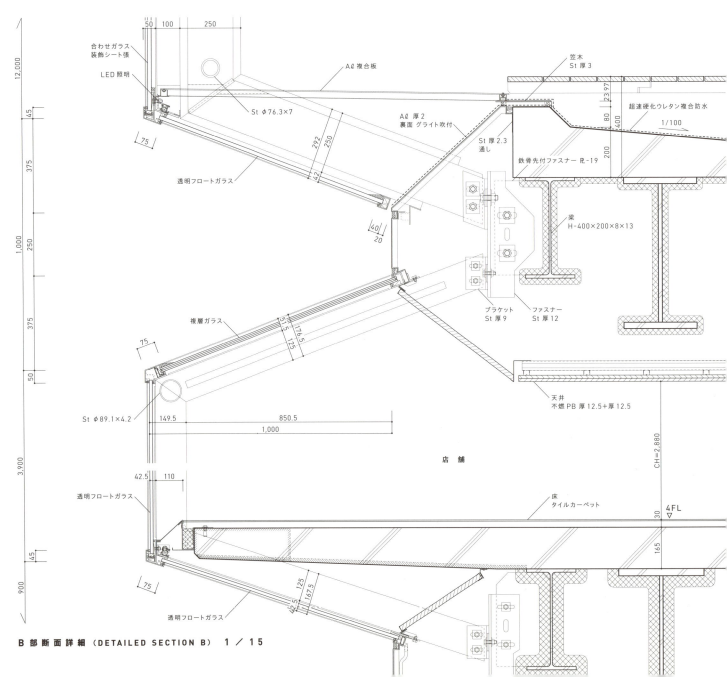

B部断面詳細（DETAILED SECTION B） 1／15

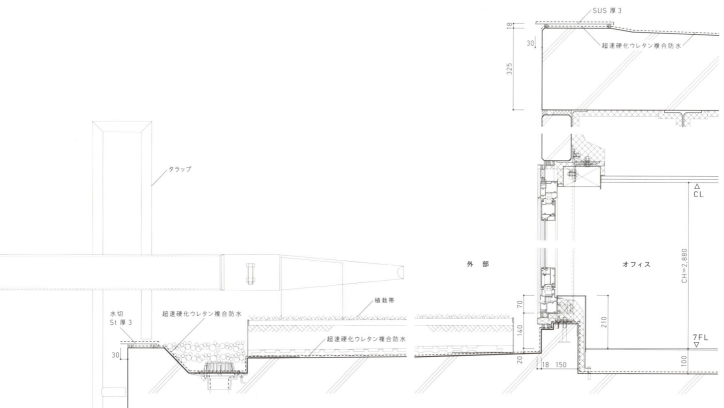

C部断面詳細 (DETAILED SECTION C)　1／15

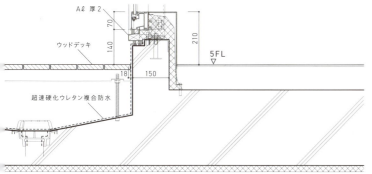

大阪・心斎橋の商業中心地に立つSPC（特別目的会社）による、商業と事務所の複合施設である。クライアントの要望は大通りの御堂筋から目立つこと、そして下階の賃料が高いフロアを最大限確保することであった。大通りから一歩入ったわずか12mの幅員の道路に面し、残り三周は隣地に接した計画地であった。下層階を最大限確保するためには天空率は使えないため、一般的な道路斜線を使い下層階4層の商業テナントと上部3層の事務所の7層を、31mの隣地斜線最大高さ以下に入れることとした。屋上階やセットバック部分のパラペットを最小限にし、周辺より競争力をもたせるために最大限の天井高さを確保することができる超速硬化ウレタン複合防水を利用した断面の提案を行った。上部3層のセットバック部のファサードはガラスの工作物とし、下部4層の上にガラスボックスの賑わいが積層したファサードとした。（三菱地所設計　須部恭浩）

This complex of commercial and office facilities employing the SPC (structured investment vehicle) method stands in the heart of Osaka's Shinsaibashi business district. The client desired a design that would stand out prominently on Midosuji boulevard while securing the maximum number of lower level floors rentable at high rates. The project site faced on a narrow 12m road, one step from the boulevard, with its remaining three sides adjoined by neighboring sites. Securing the maximum number of lower level floors meant giving up the sky factor. We therefore employed the road setback line and placed seven floors, including four lower level commercial floors, at the maximum 31m setback rule height. By minimizing the parapets on the roof and setback floors, we endeavored to make the ceilings as high as possible for a visually competitive building. This was enabled by means of a section design using a multi-component ultra fast curing polyurethane waterproofing membrane system. The facades of the four commercial floors and setbacks of the upper three floors are designed as workpieces of glass. In this way, we achieved a building of layered glass boxes animated by interior bustle and activity.
(MITSUBISHI JISHO SEKKEI INC., Yasuhiro Sube)

Roof II ———— 8

地下空間に
浮遊する，
フラットスラブの
中庭

Flat Slab Courtyard Suspended
in Underground Space

竹中大工道具館新館
竹中工務店

Takenaka Carpentry Tools Museum
Takenaka Corporation

施工：竹中工務店
構造：S造，RC造
規模：地上1階，地下2階
竣工：2014年4月
所在：兵庫県神戸市
撮影：彰国社写真部（p52, 54），古川泰造（p53, 55）

Constructor: Takenaka Corporation
Structure: S+RC
Number of stories: 1 story, 2 basements
Completion date: April, 2014
Location: Kobe-city, Hyogo
Photo: Shokokusha Photographer (p52, 54),
Taizo Furukawa (p53, 55)

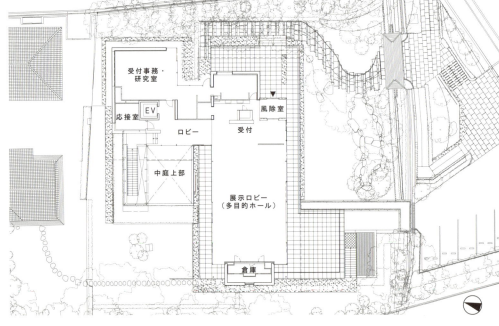

1階平面（1st FLOOR PLAN） 1／500

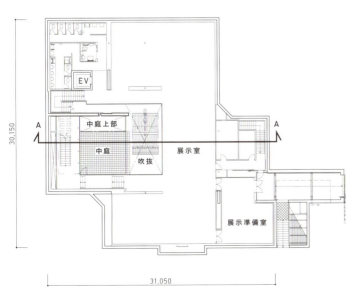

地下1階平面（B1 FLOOR PLAN） 1／500　　　　A－A断面（SECTION A-A） 1／400

竹中大工道具館新館では、地下2層にわたる常設展示空間においても、地上の豊かな緑や自然光が感じられるよう、地下1階・地下2階レベルに立体的な中庭を設けている。なかでも象徴となる地下1階レベルの中庭は、内外区画となる極薄コンクリートフラットスラブが浮遊する意匠を目指した。スラブ上部は超速硬化ウレタン複合防水の上に伝統窯で焼かれた瓦仕上げを施し、スラブ下面（地下2階天井面）はコンクリート杉板本実型枠打放し仕上げとすることで、スラブ高さ寸法を極限まで抑えた。構造体であるスラブそのものが、型枠大工のみならず防水・瓦といった他職種を含めた職人技術の結晶として表現されることを狙った。
（竹中工務店　須賀定邦）

The new wing of Takenaka Carpentry Tools Museum features an indoor courtyard on floors B1 and B2, so that visitors can enjoy the feeling of above ground greenery and natural light, even in a permanent exhibition space that spans two underground floors. In particular, the symbolic courtyard on the B1 level is designed to have ultra-thin concrete flat slabs defining the inner and exterior spaces. The upper sections of the slabs are treated with multi-component ultra fast curing polyurethane waterproofing membrane system finished with tiles baked in traditional kilns, with the undersides (the ceiling face of B2) finished in exposed concrete stamped with tongue and groove cedar boards, thereby keeping the slab height measurements to an absolute minimum. The aim was to make the structural slabs themselves an expression of the crystallization of traditional techniques, including other crafts such as waterproofing and tiles, in addition to formwork carpentry.
(Takenaka Corporation Sadakuni Suga)

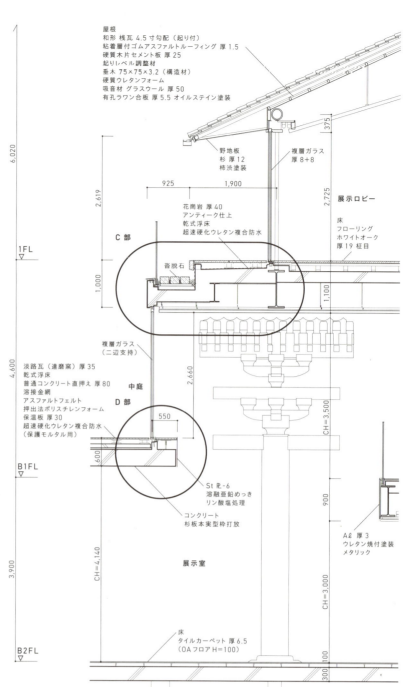

B部断面（SECTION B）　1／80

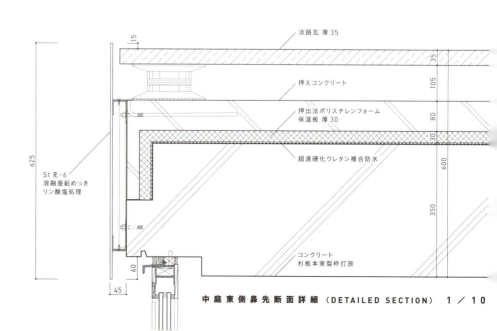

中庭東側鼻先断面詳細（DETAILED SECTION）　1／10

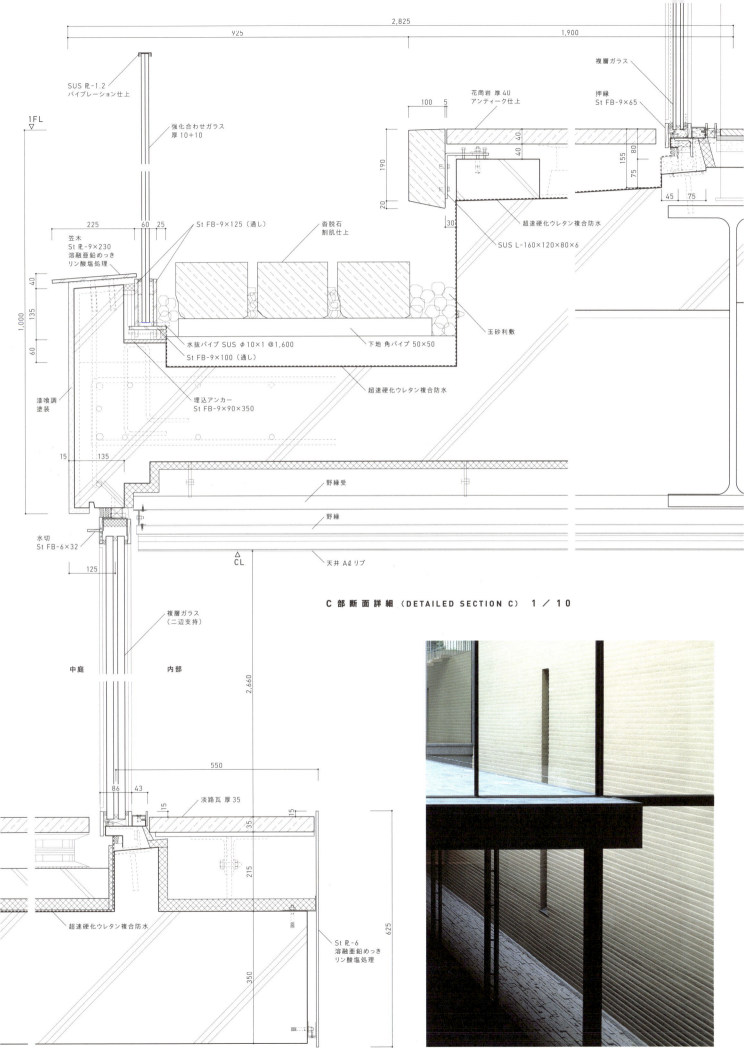

C部断面詳細 (DETAILED SECTION C) 1／10

D部断面詳細 (DETAILED SECTION D) 1／10

Curved Roof — 9

地面が浮き上がったような自由曲面屋根

A Free-form Roof
—as if the Ground Had Risen

川口市めぐりの森
伊東豊雄建築設計事務所

'Meguri no Mori'
Kawaguchi City Funeral Hall
Toyo Ito & Associates, Architects

施工：東亜・埼和特定建設工事共同企業体
型枠工事：キヤマ（設計），堀江製函合板所（製作）
カーテンウォール工事：ニュースト
構造：RC造，一部S造
規模：地上2階，地下1階
竣工：2017年12月
所在：埼玉県川口市
撮影：中村絵（p56）
写真提供：伊東豊雄建築設計事務所（p58, 59）

Constructor: Toa, Saiwa JV
Form work: Kiyama Corp., (designing),
HORIE SEIKAN GOUHANSYO.CO.LTD（molding）
Curtain wall work: NEWXT
Structure: RC+S
Number of stories: 2 stories, 1 basement
Completion date: December, 2017
Location: Kawaguchi-city, Saitama
Photo: Kai Nakamura (p56)
Courtesy of: Toyo Ito & Associates, Architects
(p58, 59)

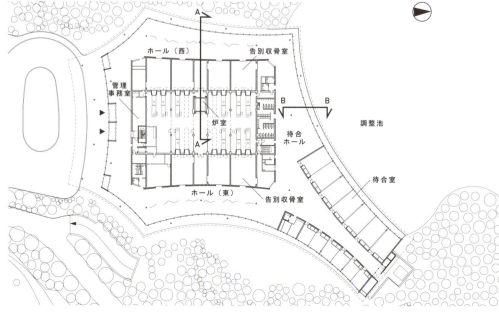

1階平面（1st FLOOR PLAN） 1／1,200

56　DETAIL extra issue

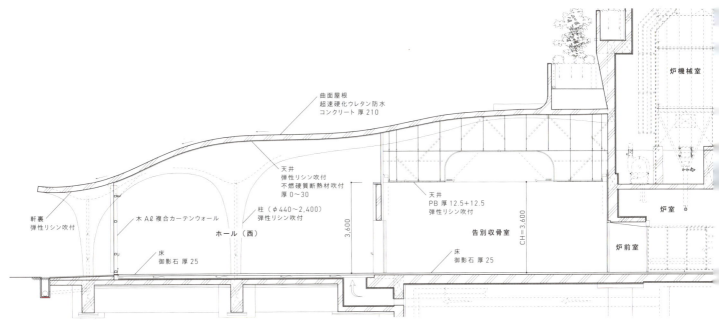

A－A断面（SECTION A-A） 1／150

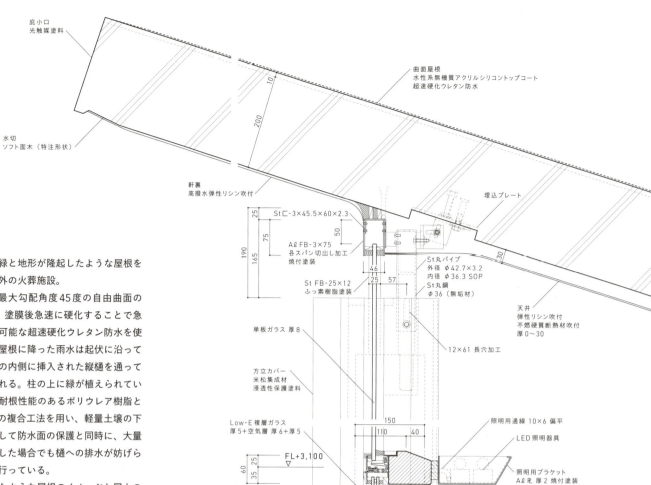

C部断面詳細（DETAILED SECTION C） 1／8

周囲の公園の緑と地形が隆起したような屋根をもつ川口市郊外の火葬施設。

厚さ200mm最大勾配角度45度の自由曲面のRC屋根には、塗膜後急速に硬化することで急勾配にも施工可能な超速硬化ウレタン防水を使用している。屋根に降った雨水は起伏に沿って流れ、鉄骨柱の内側に挿入された縦樋を通って外部に排水される。柱の上に緑が植えられている部分には、耐根性能のあるポリウレア樹脂とウレタン防水の複合工法を用い、軽量土壌の下を二重構造として防水面の保護と同時に、大量に雨水が流入した場合でも樋への排水が妨げられない配慮を行っている。

地面が隆起したような屋根のイメージと屋上の立ち上がり部分のれんがタイルとの意匠的な一体性を実現するため、屋根部分の防水面の保護材には、土に近い質感でかつ靴底に対する摩擦力が大きく安全性の高い無機系の保護材を使用し、特注色のサンプルを何度も作製してタイルに近い質感と色を追求した。

（伊東豊雄建築設計事務所　林盛）

This roof of this crematorium in the outskirts of Kawaguchi evokes the image of a rising and falling landform. The 200mm-thick RC roof has a maximum incline angle of 45 degrees. On such a roof, we used an ultra fast curing polyurethane waterproofing membrane, applicable even on steep pitches because it hardens so quickly after application. Rainwater falling on the roof drains along the slopes and passes through vertical drain pipes, inserted in the steel pillars, to be expelled outside.

On portions above the pillars where greenery is planted, we used a compound of polyurea resin and polyurethane waterproofing membrane having strong resistance to root penetration. While enabling a two-layer waterproofing structure beneath the lightweight soil, it ensures that drainage into the drain pipes will not be impeded even under large quantities of rainwater.

In order to realize visual unity between the roof's image of rising and falling land and the brick tile of the rooftop's raised elements, we employed an inorganic protective material close in character to soil on the roof waterproofing. The protective material also offers resistance to the soles of shoes for enhanced safety. We repeatedly had custom color samples created in our pursuit of a material close in character and color to the tile. (Toyo Ito & Associates, Architects Sei Hayashi)

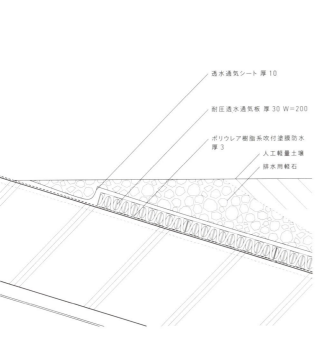

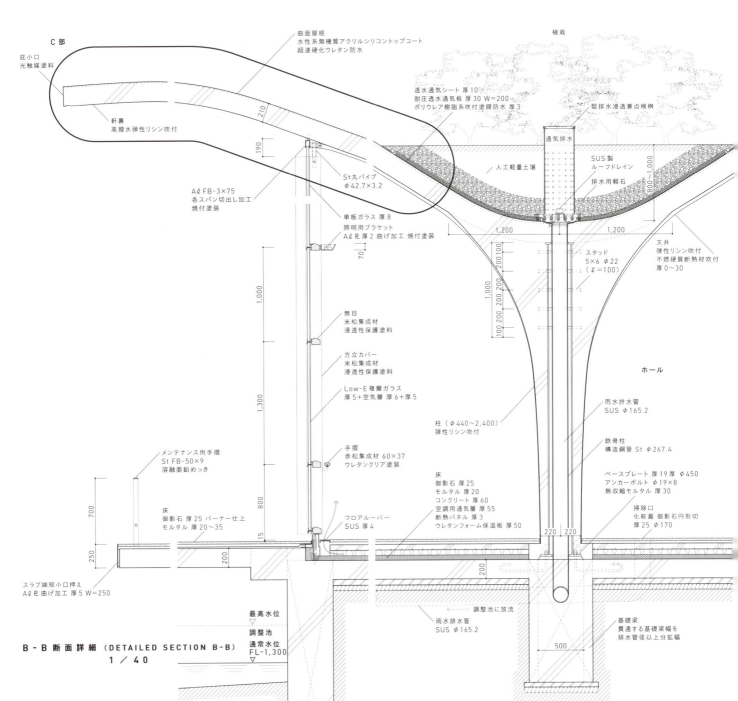

B−B断面詳細（DETAILED SECTION B-B）
1／40

Curved Roof — 10

9mm厚の鉄板による円筒シェルの防水

Waterproofing a Cylindrical Shell Made of 9mm-thick Steel Panels

アストラムライン新白島駅
小嶋一浩＋赤松佳珠子／CAt，
パシフィックコンサルタンツ

Astramline Shin-hakushima Station
Kazuhiro Kojima + Kazuko Akamatsu / CAt,
PACIFIC CONSULTANTS CO., LTD.

施工：フジタ・栗本建設工事共同企業体，河崎組，
プランニング三誠
構造：S造
規模：地上1階，地下1階
竣工：2015年10月
所在：広島県広島市
写真提供：CAt

Constructor: Fujita and Kurimoto Construction JV, Kawasakigumi, Planning Sansei
Structure: S
Number of stories: 1 story, 1 basement
Completion date: October, 2015
Location: Hiroshima-city, Hiroshima
Courtesy of: CAt

断面（SECTION） 1／800

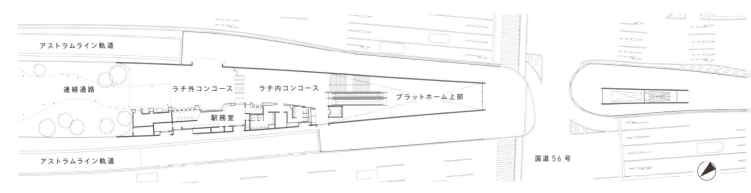

平面（PLAN） 1／800

新白島駅は広島市の新交通システム・アストラムラインとJR山陽本線との乗換え駅の計画である。敷地は片側3車線の国道の中州に位置する。昼夜問わず激しい自動車交通を考慮し、新駅と国道との間にバッファーとなるよう円筒状のシェルを提案、9mmの鉄板の外側に12mmのフラットバーのリブを溶接する構造となった。

山陽本線のプラットホームは2階、アストラムラインのプラットホームは地下1階に位置していたため、当初から一貫して、地上と地下を一体的につなぐ要素として円筒シェルを構想していた。内側は鉄板そのままの仕上げとすることができたが、外側はリブとリブとの間の溝を埋め、その上に防水を施す構法が必要となった。また、防水端末納まりにインサート取手、シェルガラス窓、立上り、ケラバ等があり、これらへの対応も防水上の課題であった。

意匠的には、できるだけ目地や凹凸のないシームレスな外観を目指していた中で、詳細設計を担当していたパシフィックコンサルタンツから提案されたのが、恒常的に粘性のある追従型のシート防水と圧縮空気混合超速硬化ウレタン防水による二重防水である。

これらによって、3次元的に複雑な円筒シェルの形態を問題なく一体的に仕上げることが可能となった。また、とりわけ施工上問題だったのは、屋根と壁が一体化しているゆえに、勾配が非常に急な箇所が発生することであったが、圧縮空気混合超速硬化ウレタン防水工法は、急勾配の下地にも均一な膜厚の確保が可能であった。（CAt　有井敦生（元所員））

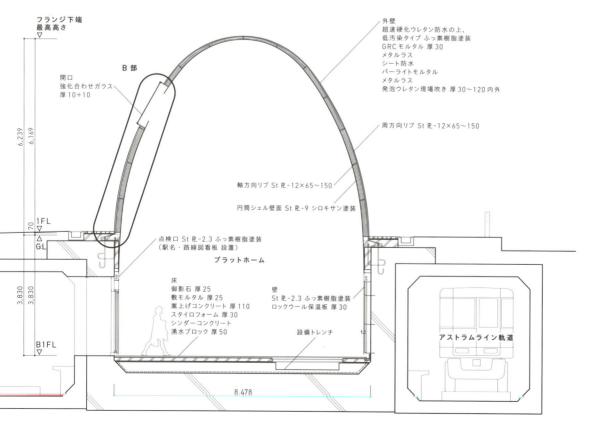

A−A断面（SECTION A-A）　1／120

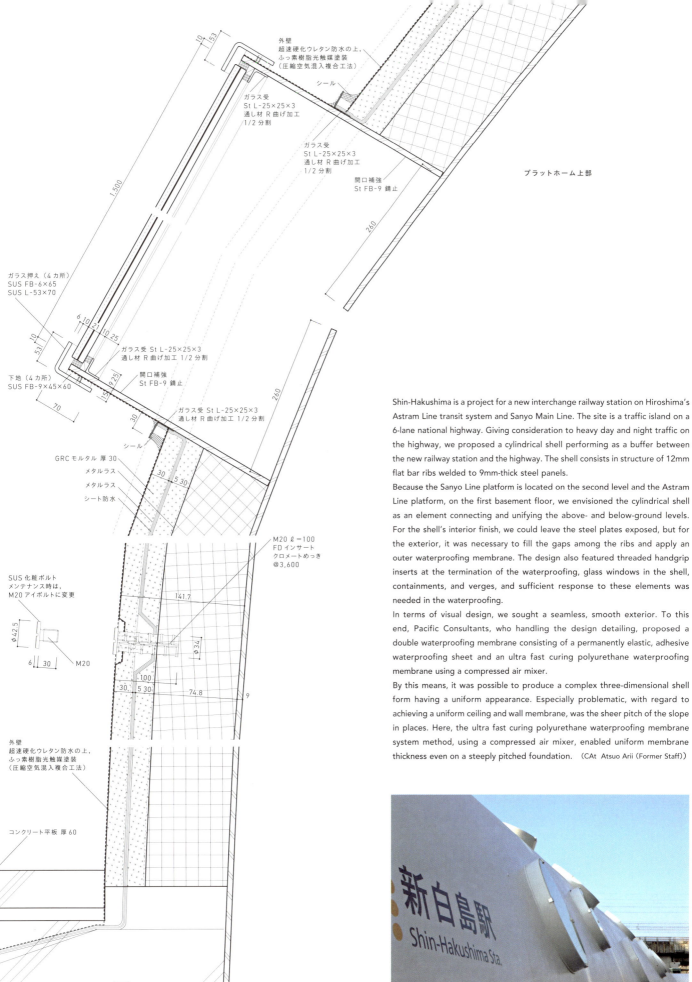

Shin-Hakushima is a project for a new interchange railway station on Hiroshima's Astram Line transit system and Sanyo Main Line. The site is a traffic island on a 6-lane national highway. Giving consideration to heavy day and night traffic on the highway, we proposed a cylindrical shell performing as a buffer between the new railway station and the highway. The shell consists in structure of 12mm flat bar ribs welded to 9mm-thick steel panels.

Because the Sanyo Line platform is located on the second level and the Astram Line platform, on the first basement floor, we envisioned the cylindrical shell as an element connecting and unifying the above- and below-ground levels. For the shell's interior finish, we could leave the steel plates exposed, but for the exterior, it was necessary to fill the gaps among the ribs and apply an outer waterproofing membrane. The design also featured threaded handgrip inserts at the termination of the waterproofing, glass windows in the shell, containments, and verges, and sufficient response to these elements was needed in the waterproofing.

In terms of visual design, we sought a seamless, smooth exterior. To this end, Pacific Consultants, who handling the design detailing, proposed a double waterproofing membrane consisting of a permanently elastic, adhesive waterproofing sheet and an ultra fast curing polyurethane waterproofing membrane using a compressed air mixer.

By this means, it was possible to produce a complex three-dimensional shell form having a uniform appearance. Especially problematic, with regard to achieving a uniform ceiling and wall membrane, was the sheer pitch of the slope in places. Here, the ultra fast curing polyurethane waterproofing membrane system method, using a compressed air mixer, enabled uniform membrane thickness even on a steeply pitched foundation.　(CAt Atsuo Arii (Former Staff))

B部断面詳細（DETAILED SECTION B）　1／6

Curved Roof **11**

タイル葺きの
RC曲面屋根と
緑化帯

A Tiled RC Curved Roof with
Green Roofing

**多治見市
モザイクタイルミュージアム**
藤森照信＋
エイ・ケイ設計＋エース設計共同体

Mosaic Tile Museum, Tajimi
Terunobu Fujimori,
Space Design Office ak-sekkei,
Ace Design Comunity

施工：吉川・加藤・桜井特定建設工事共同企業体
構造：RC造
規模：地上4階
竣工：2016年3月
所在：岐阜県多治見市
写真提供：元旦ビューティ工業

Constructor: Yoshikawa, Kato, Sakurai JV
Structure: RC
Number of stories: 4 stories
Completion date: March, 2016
Location: Tajimi-city, Gifu
Courtesy of: Gantan Beauty Industry Co., Ltd.

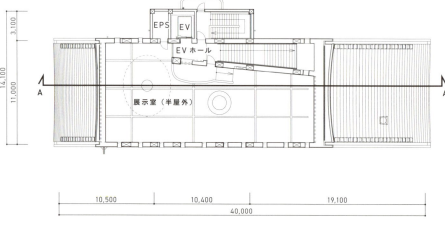

4階平面（4th FLOOR PLAN）　1／400

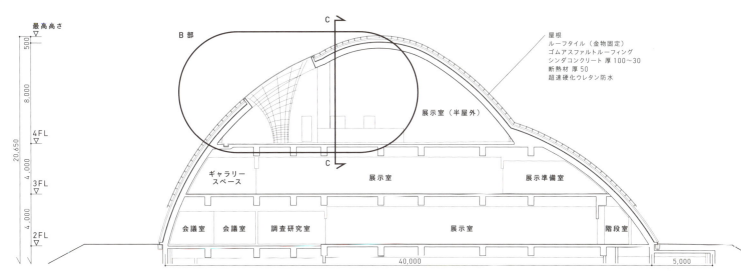

A-A 断面 (SECTION A-A) 1／300

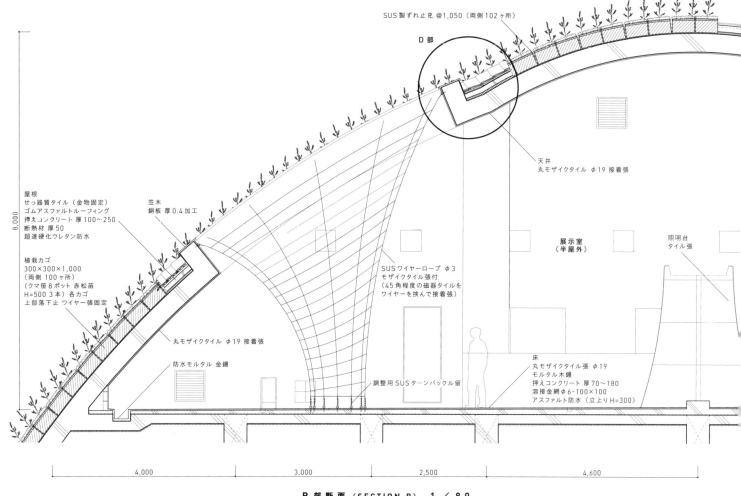

B部断面（SECTION B） 1／80

藤森照信氏が当初よりイメージしていた曲面の屋根を実現するには、シート防水やアスファルト防水では施工上の困難が予想されたので、防水業者と相談のうえ超速硬化ウレタン防水を採用した。超速硬化ウレタン防水は、専用のスプレーで塗布後、数十秒で硬化し始める特徴があり、曲面や傾斜にもシームレスで施工を行うことができるので今回の建物には適当であった。また当初は全面的に屋上緑化を行う予定だったが、コストとメンテナンス上の都合から、屋根の両端だけに植栽帯を設けた。そこには耐植物性バクテリアや耐根性に優れたポリウレアを超速硬化ウレタン防水の上から行っている。中央部のタイル屋根は、超速硬化ウレタン防水を行った後、押えコンクリートを打ち、そこに引っ掛け金物を取り付けてタイル屋根を葺いている。
（エイ・ケイ設計 水野秀利）

In realizing the curved roof envisioned by Fujimori Terunobu, difficulties in applying sheet or asphalt waterproofing were foreseen. After consulting a waterproofing contractor, we employed an ultra fast curing polyurethane waterproofing membrane system.
The ultra fast curing polyurethane waterproofing membrane begins setting in less than a minute after its application with a sprayer. Because it can be applied seamlessly to a curved or pitched surface, the method suited this building well. Originally, the plan was to greenify the entire roof, but owing to budget and maintenance limitations, strips of vegetation were established only at the edges of the roof. Under them—and over the ultra fast curing polyurethane waterproofing membrane—we applied polyurea strongly resistant to plant bacteria and root penetration. To create the central tiled roof portion, we applied an ultra fast curing polyurethane waterproofing membrane then poured a protective concrete layer, attached roof hooks, and tiled the roof surface.
(Space Design Office ak-sekkei Hidetoshi Mizuno)

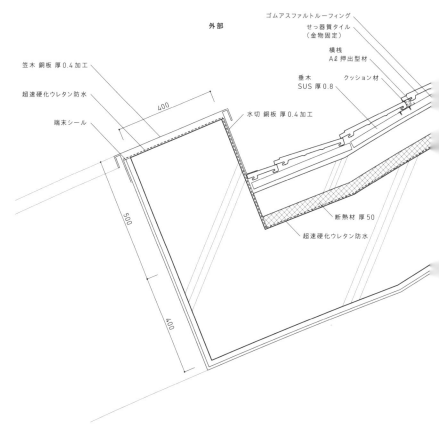

D部断面詳細（DETAILED SECTION D） 1／15

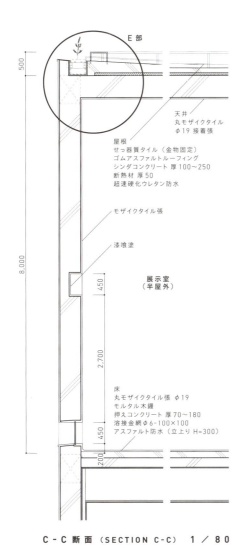

C-C断面（SECTION C-C） 1／80

天井
丸モザイクタイル
φ19 接着張

屋根
せっ器質タイル（金物固定）
ゴムアスファルトルーフィング
シンダコンクリート 厚100～250
断熱材 厚50
超速硬化ウレタン防水

モザイクタイル張

漆喰塗

展示室
（半屋外）

床
丸モザイクタイル張 φ19
モルタル木鏝
押えコンクリート 厚70～180
溶接金網φ6-100×100
アスファルト防水（立上り H=300）

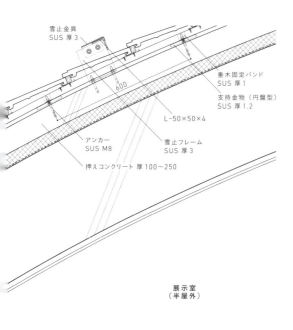

雪止金具
SUS 厚3

垂木固定バンド
SUS 厚1

支持金物（円盤型）
SUS 厚1.2

L-50×50×4

アンカー
SUS M8

雪止フレーム
SUS 厚3

押えコンクリート 厚100～250

展示室
（半屋外）

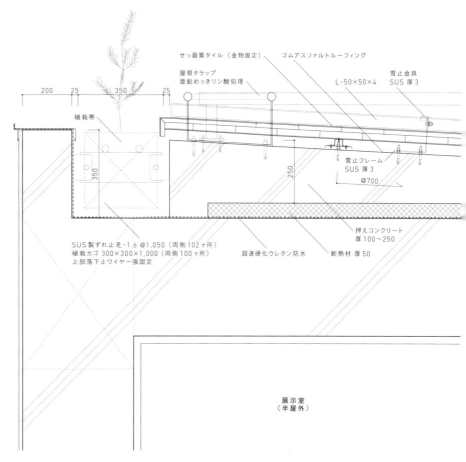

E部断面詳細（DETAILED SECTION E） 1／15

植栽帯

屋根タラップ
亜鉛めっきリン酸処理

せっ器質タイル（金物固定）　ゴムアスファルトルーフィング

雪止金具
SUS 厚3

L-50×50×4

雪止フレーム
SUS 厚3
@700

押えコンクリート
厚100～250

超速硬化ウレタン防水　断熱材 厚50

SUS製ずれ止凡-1.6 @1,050（両側102ヶ所）
植栽カゴ 300×300×1,000（両側100ヶ所）
上部落下止ワイヤー張固定

展示室
（半屋外）

Curved Roof 12

洞窟状の空間を自由に覆う防水膜

Freely Applicable
Waterproofing Membrane
for a Cavernous Space

台中国家歌劇院
伊東豊雄建築設計事務所・
大矩聯合建築師事務所

National Taichung Theater
Toyo Ito & Associates, Architects,
DA-JU Architects & Associates

施工：麗明營造
舞台設備工事：台大丰・金樹營造共同企業体
構造：RC造，一部S造
規模：地上6階，地下2階，塔屋1階
竣工：2016年9月
所在：台湾台中市
撮影：畠山直哉（p68）
写真提供：伊東豊雄建築設計事務所（p71）

Constructor: Lee Ming Construction Co., LTD
Specialized Stage Equipment:
Top Design Futurity International Co., LTD.,
Chin Shu Construction Company LTD. JV
Structure: RC+S
Number of stories: 6 stories, 2 basements,
1 rooftop structure
Completion date: September, 2016
Location: Taichung-city, Taiwan
Photo: Naoya Hatakeyama（p68），
Courtesy of: Toyo Ito & Associates, Architects
（p71）

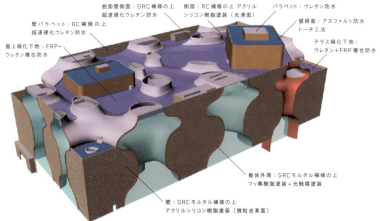

防水仕様ゾーニング
（Zoning of Waterproofs）

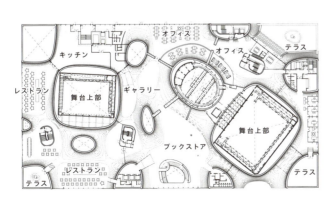

5階平面（5th FLOOR PLAN）
1／1,500

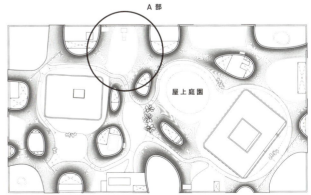

6階平面（6th FLOOR PLAN）
1／1,500

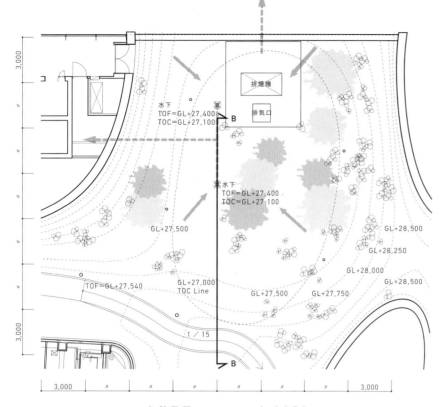

A部平面（PLAN A） 1／250

台中国家歌劇院は、複雑な3次元曲面RC構造による巨大な洞窟状の空間を特徴とする。
この空間には、大中小三つの劇場をはじめ、商業テナントスペース、ギャラリー、パブリックスペースなどが内包されている。
洞窟状の空間には、テラスなどの屋外空間も立体的に挿入されているため、その場所の適性に応じた種類の防水が選ばれている。
フライタワー上部などフラットな面には、アスファルト防水・トーチ工法。緑化面には、植物の根に対し耐久性のあるウレタン＋FRP複合防水。そして3次元曲面には、自由度の高い超速硬化ウレタン防水が選定された。
ウレタン＋FRP複合防水と超速硬化ウレタン防水については実績のある日本メーカーが採用された。屋上の床から壁にかけてその2種類の防水が切り替わる部分では、ふかしモルタルで10cmの垂直な立上りをつくり、防水を重ね合わせることで、3次元曲面と緑化面がスムーズにつながるようなディテールを実現した。
（伊東豊雄建築設計事務所　藤江航）

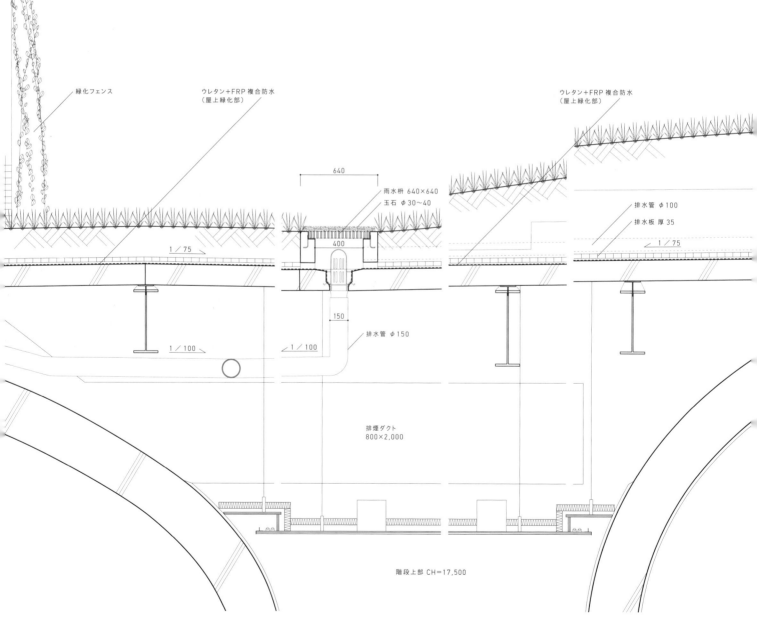

B-B断面詳細（DETAILED SECTION B-B） 1／30

The National Taichung Theater is distinguished by a cavernous space, realized using a complex three-dimensional curved RC structure. The space contains three theaters—large, medium, and small—along with commercial tenant space, galleries, and public space. Because terraces and other exterior spaces penetrate the interior of the cavernous space three-dimensionally, the most suitable waterproofing method was chosen for the needs of each location. The torch-applied asphalt waterproofing method was employed for the flat surfaces above the fly tower and such. For the greenified surfaces, a polyurethane + FRP multi-component waterproofing membrane having strong resistance to root penetration was used. Then, for vertical surfaces, a multi-component ultra fast curing polyurethane waterproofing membrane system enabling a high-degree of freedom was chosen. We located a Japanese manufacturer with good credentials for a polyurethane + FRP multi-component waterproofing membrane and ultra fast curing polyurethane waterproofing membrane systems. At areas of transition from the roof floor to wall where the two membranes converge, we created a 10cm vertical containment using leveling mortar, then overlapped the membranes at the containment for a sealed transition from the wall to the vegetation cover. (Toyo Ito & Associates, Architects Wataru Fujie)

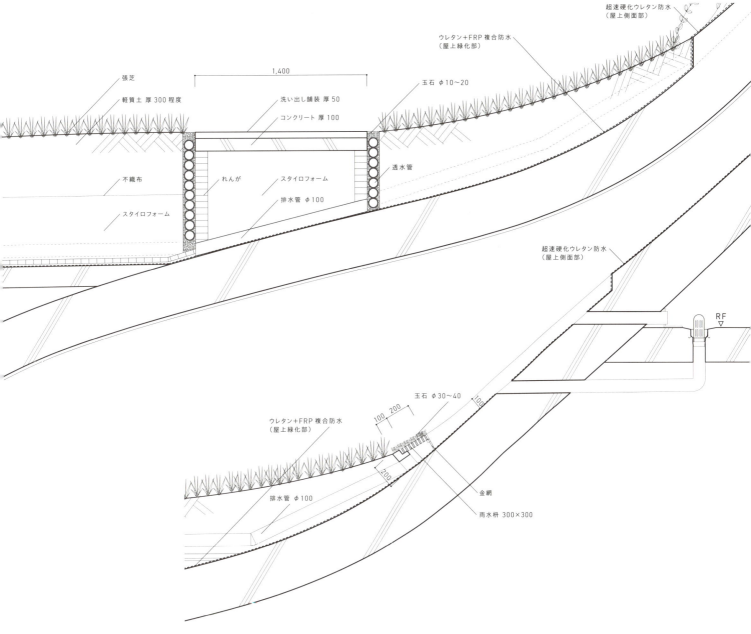

排水口部断面詳細（DETAILED SECTION） 1／30

Roof + Cladding 13

機能性と意匠性を兼ね備えた屋上
Rooftop Providing a Combination of Functionality and Design

青森県立美術館
青木淳建築計画事務所

Aomori Museum of Art
JUN AOKI & ASSOCIATES

施工：竹中・西松・奥村・北斗特定建設共同企業体
構造：SRC造，S造
規模：地上3階，地下2階
竣工：2005年9月
所在：青森県青森市
撮影：彰国社写真部（p72，74下）
写真提供：青森県立美術館（p74上）

Constructor: Takenaka, Nishimatsu, Okumura, and Hokuto JV
Structure: SRC+S
Number of stories: 3 stories, 2 basements
Completion date: September, 2005
Location: Aomori-city, Aomori
Photo: Shokokusha Photographer (p72, 74lower)
Courtesy of: Aomori Museum of Art (p74upper)

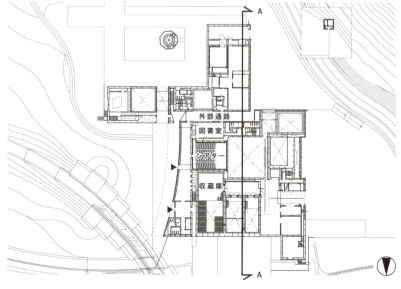

1階平面（1st FLOOR PLAN） 1／2,000

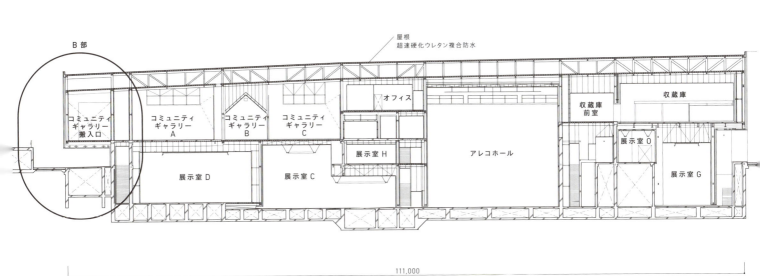

A-A断面（SECTION A-A） 1／600

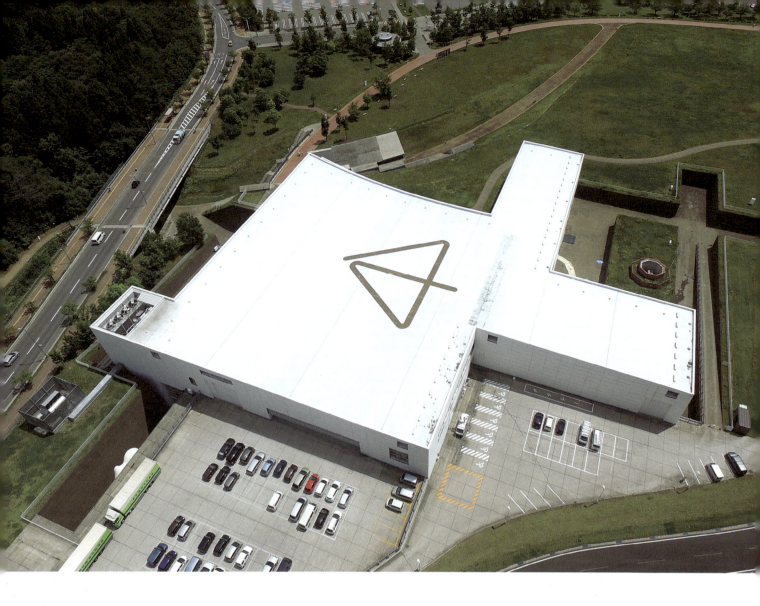

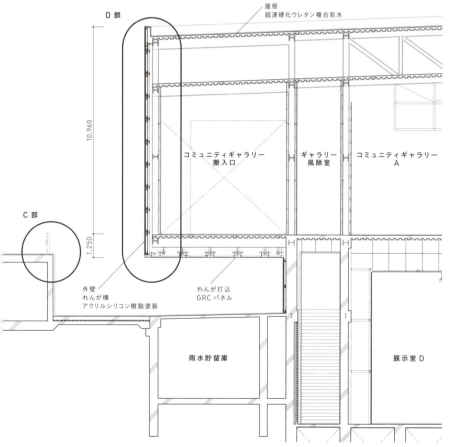

B部矩計（SECTION B） 1／200

美術館の屋上であることから、万が一の場合に改修が容易であること、屋上面積が大きいために押えコンクリートの採用は荷重の面から望ましくないなどの機能的要請により、通気緩衝シートを用いた超速硬化ウレタン複合防水を採用した。それによって、外壁に合わせたトップコートの白塗装をすることが可能となり、日射熱の影響を最小限にとどめることができた。また、当時はgoogle Earthが使われ始めたころで、今後建物を上空から見る視点が重要となると思われたこと、青森空港が近いため航空機から美術館が視認できることから、巨大なロゴマークを屋上にペイントする案が浮上した。したがって、防水層の上にペイントが可能であるという意匠への展開性の高さも採用の大きな契機となった。

（青木淳建築計画事務所　西澤徹夫（元所員））

Being the roof of an art gallery, there were functional demands, such as ease of repair in the event of an emergency, and the need to keep down the weight of the concrete overlay due to the large surface area of the roof, so an environmentally friendly composite waterproofing mechanical fastening method was used, featuring a multi-component ultra fast curing polyurethane waterproofing membrane system. This meant that the top coat could be painted white, matching the outer walls and keeping the effects of solar radiation to a minimum. Also, since Google Earth had just started around that time, it was felt that it would be important for the structure to be visible from above in the future, and, since Aomori Airport is close, the idea was proposed that a huge logo should be painted on the roof, so that the museum could be identified from an aircraft. It was also a major opportunity to adopt the design potential of being able to paint on top of the waterproofing layer.

(JUN AOKI & ASSOCIATES Tetsuo Nishizawa (Former Staff))

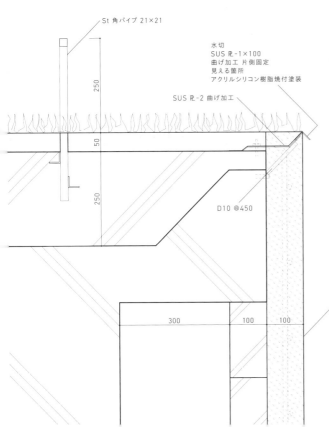
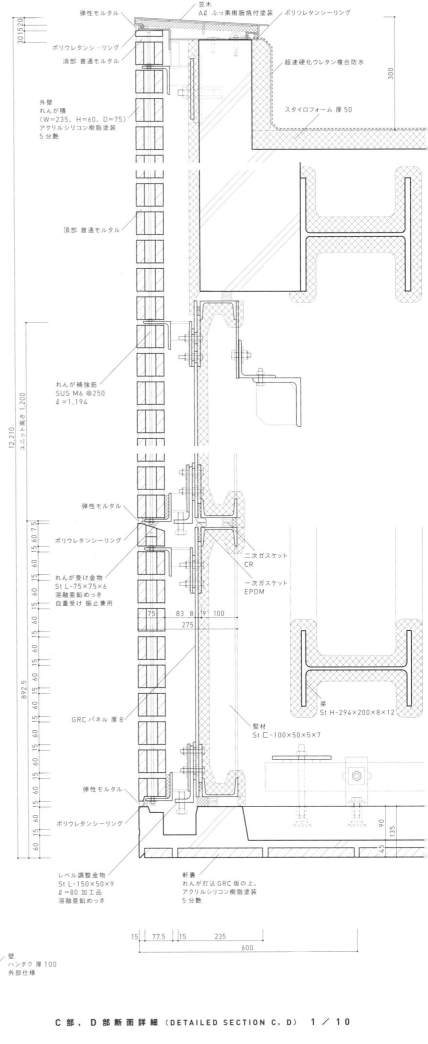

C部, D部断面詳細 (DETAILED SECTION C, D)　1／10

Roof + Cladding **14**

建物高さを抑えた，アルミ水平ルーバーのファサード

Aluminum Horizontal Louver Facade Reduces Sense of Height of Building

東北学院大学 土樋キャンパス ホーイ記念館
三菱地所設計

Tohoku Gakuin University Tsuchitoi Campus Hoy Memorial Hall
MITSUBISHI JISHO SEKKEI INC.

施工：大林組
構造：S造，一部RC造
規模：地上5階，地下1階
竣工：2016年3月
所在：宮城県仙台市
撮影：解良信介

Constructor: OBAYASHI CORPORATION
Structure: S+RC
Number of stories: 5 stories, 1 basement
Completion date: March, 2016
Location: Sendai-city, Miyagi
Photo: Shinsuke Kera

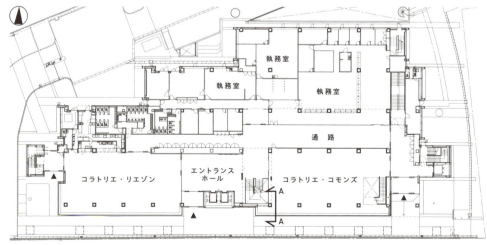

1階平面（1st FLOOR PLAN） 1／800

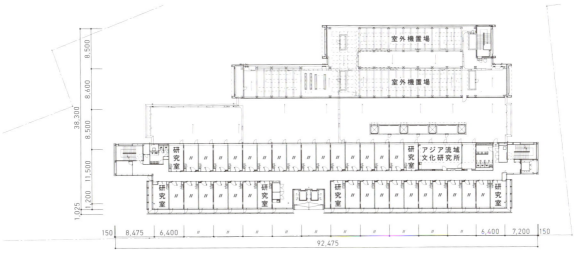

4階平面（4th FLOOR PLAN） 1／800

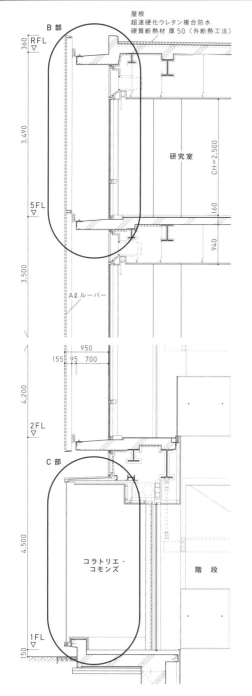

A-A矩計（SECTION A-A） 1／80

東北学院大学 ホーイ記念館は、講義室、研究室、ラーニングコモンズ等を有した、地下1階・地上5階、延床面積12,748㎡の建物である。研究室や講義室の開口部に配された簾のようなアルミ水平ルーバーは、通りの人々からの視線を遮るとともに、室内を優しい光で満たす。

このホーイ記念館は住宅地に隣接するキャンパス内にあるため、延床面積10,000㎡を超える建物を配棟するには、街並みへの配慮が必要であり、何より建物高さを抑えることが大事なポイントであると考えた。多目的ホールを地下に配置するなど、計画的な側面から建物ボリュームを抑える努力を重ねることはもちろんのこと、超速硬化ウレタン複合防水を採用することで、一般的なアゴ付きのパラペット形状よりもパラペットを低く計画することが可能となり、このことも高さを抑えたファサードを形成することに大きく寄与している。（三菱地所設計　大林敬幸）

Tohoku Gakuin University's Hoy Memorial Hall houses lecture rooms, laboratories and a learning commons, etc., in five floors above ground and one basement, with a total floor area of 12,748㎡. The aluminum horizontal louver slats arranged in front of the entrances to the lecture rooms and laboratories shield the interior from the gaze of passers-by, and fill the rooms with gentle light.

The Hoy Memorial Hall is sited on campus adjacent to a residential area, so it was necessary that the buildings and over 10,000㎡ of space blend harmoniously with the surrounding area. In particular, it was important to keep the building from seeming too high. Naturally, many efforts were made to reduce the physical volume of the building, such as by putting the multi-purpose hall underground, etc., and, by using multi-component ultra fast curing polyurethane waterproofing membrane system, we were able to keep the parapet height lower than the conventional collared parapet, and this contributed significantly to reducing the sense of height of the facade.
(MITSUBISHI JISHO SEKKEI INC.　Takayuki Obayashi)

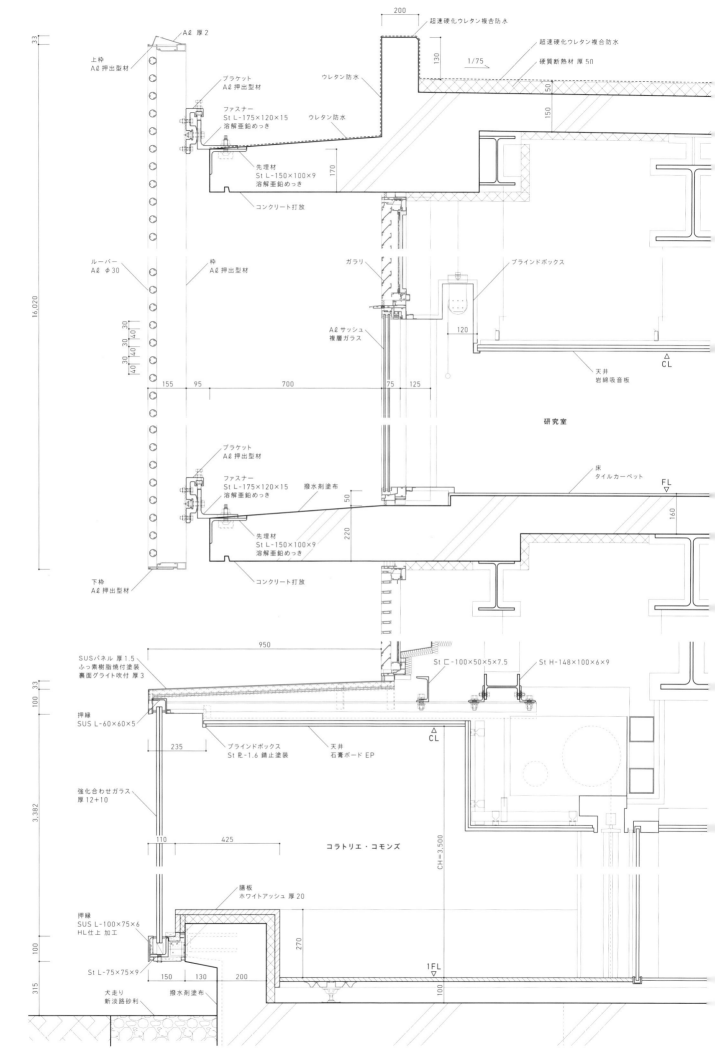

B・C部断面詳細（DETAILED SECTION B・C） 1/15

Roof + Cladding **15**

一筆書きの排水溝とケラバ部の防水

Single-stroke Drainage Channel
and Verge Waterproofing

**本郷台キリスト教会
チャーチスクール・保育園**
保坂猛建築都市設計事務所／保坂猛

Hongodai Christcharch School & Nursery
TAKESHI HOSAKA ARCHITECTS / TAKESHI HOSAKA

施工：栄港建設
構造：木造，一部Ｓ造
規模：地上２階
竣工：2010年２月
所在：神奈川県横浜市
撮影：彰国社写真部

Constructor: EIKOU KENSETSU
Structure: W+S
Number of stories: 2 stories
Completion date: February, 2010
Location: Yokohama-city, Kanagawa
Photo: Shokokusha Photographer

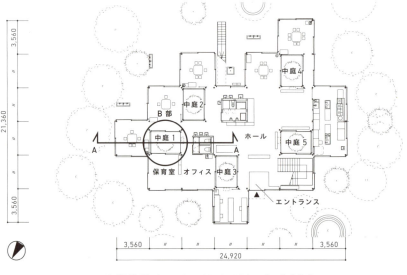

１階平面（1st FLOOR PLAN） １／400

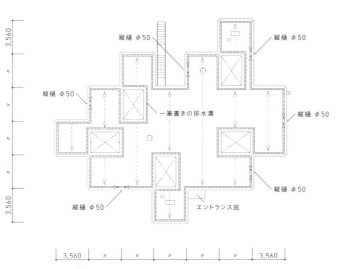

屋根伏（ROOF PLAN） 1／400

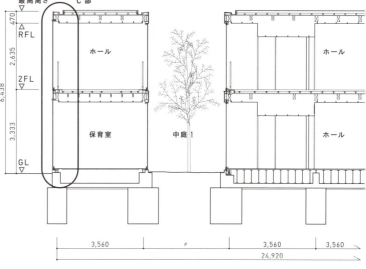

A－A断面（SECTION A-A） 1／150

木造フレーム（WOOD FRAME）

鉄骨フレーム（STEEL FRAME）

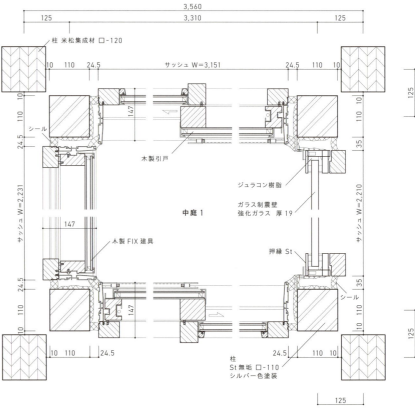

B部平面詳細（DETAILED PLAN B） 1／10

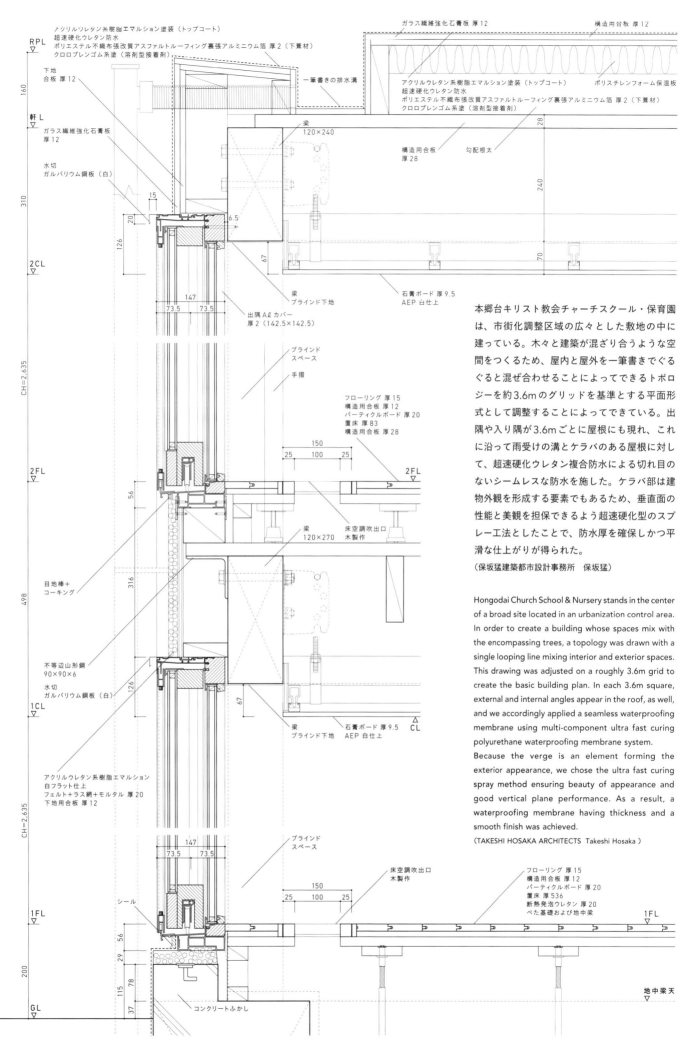

本郷台キリスト教会チャーチスクール・保育園は、市街化調整区域の広々とした敷地の中に建っている。木々と建築が混ざり合うような空間をつくるため、屋内と屋外を一筆書きでぐるぐると混ぜ合わせることによってできるトポロジーを約3.6mのグリッドを基準とする平面形式として調整することによってできている。出隅や入り隅が3.6mごとに屋根にも現れ、これに沿って雨受けの溝とケラバのある屋根に対して、超速硬化ウレタン複合防水による切れ目のないシームレスな防水を施した。ケラバ部は建物外観を形成する要素でもあるため、垂直面の性能と美観を担保できるよう超速硬化型のスプレー工法としたことで、防水厚を確保しかつ平滑な仕上がりが得られた。
（保坂猛建築都市設計事務所　保坂猛）

Hongodai Church School & Nursery stands in the center of a broad site located in an urbanization control area. In order to create a building whose spaces mix with the encompassing trees, a topology was drawn with a single looping line mixing interior and exterior spaces. This drawing was adjusted on a roughly 3.6m grid to create the basic building plan. In each 3.6m square, external and internal angles appear in the roof, as well, and we accordingly applied a seamless waterproofing membrane using multi-component ultra fast curing polyurethane waterproofing membrane system.
Because the verge is an element forming the exterior appearance, we chose the ultra fast curing spray method ensuring beauty of appearance and good vertical plane performance. As a result, a waterproofing membrane having thickness and a smooth finish was achieved.
(TAKESHI HOSAKA ARCHITECTS Takeshi Hosaka)

C部断面詳細（DETAILED SECTION C）1／8

Balcony ── 16

スラブ上の
多様な状況を
自然に成立させる

Engendering Wide-ranging
Situations on a Concrete Slab

流山市立おおたかの森小・中学校
小嶋一浩＋赤松佳珠子／CAt

Nagareyama Otakanomori Elementary
and Junior High School
Kazuhiro Kojima + Kazuko Akamatsu / CAt

施工：大林組
構造：RC造，一部PCaPC造・S造
規模：地上3階
竣工：2015年2月
所在：千葉県流山市
撮影：吉田誠（p84下，86）
写真提供：CAt（p84上）

Constructor: OBAYASHI CORPORATION
Structure: RC+PCaPC+S
Number of stories: 3 stories
Completion date: February, 2015
Location: Nagareyama-city, Chiba
Photo: Makoto Yoshida (p82lower, 84)
Courtesy of: CAt (p82upper)

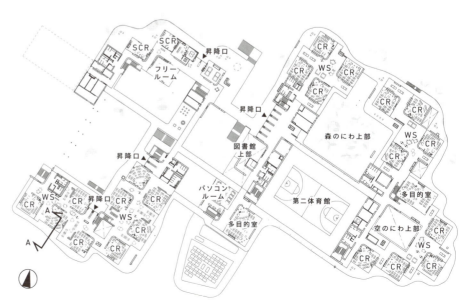

3階平面（3rd FLOOR PLAN） 1／1,500

最大約1,800人の子供たちが通う小・中学校併設校と地域交流センター・こども図書館・学童保育所が集う、約22,000㎡の大規模な複合施設である。

大きな平面のスラブがズレながら積層するなかにどのように分散して雨樋を通し、それが空間の開放性を妨げずにシンプルな構成に見せられるかがポイントであった。屋内運動場前のデッキスペースやブリッジ状のデッキスペースなど、大スパン部分であまり雨樋を落としにくい箇所では、軒樋形状（水下）になり、スラブの重なりにより縦樋が落ちてくる教室廻りのゾーンの軒先はパラペット形状になっている。それらの箇所に超速硬化ウレタン複合防水を採用することで、水の流れによって異なる様々なディテールや、軒先の見つけ寸法を統一的に見せることができた。

また、超速硬化ウレタン複合防水は様々な取合いが発生する場合にも納まりの自由度が高く、施工性が良いのが特徴であるが、デッキスペースに配置された菜園やベンチ、手洗い場などの多岐にわたる納まりが、デッキ下の限られたスペースの中で1つの種類の防水で完結している。大きなデッキスペースの上は、デッキ下での出来事はなかったかのように、子どもたちのイキイキとしたアクティビティが自然と広がっている。（CAt　大村真也）

The project is a building complex, some 22,000㎡ in scale, that includes a combined elementary and junior-school school for some 1,800 children and a combined regional exchange center, children's library, and after-school day-care center.

How to pass drain pipes through the large offset slabs without blocking the open spaces, so as to present a composition of simple appearance, became one important issue. The eaves of the slab take the form of gutters in areas of broad span where a drain pipe would hamper activity, such as deck spaces near interior classroom activity areas and bridge-type deck spaces. In places where the slabs overlap with one another and drain pipes are easily placeable, such as zones around classrooms, we installed a parapet at the edge of the slab. By using multi-component ultra fast curing polyurethane waterproofing membrane system in all these places, we could give a unified appearance to the varying details governing water drainage and the varying dimensions of the eaves.

The multi-component ultra fast curing polyurethane waterproofing membrane system is distinguished by the freedom and ease with which it can be applied in situations where diverse fittings are employed. In the limited space below each deck, whose upper surface hosts varied vegetable gardens, benches, and wash places, a single waterproofing method could be used. As a result, on each large deck slab, children's activities unfold naturally, oblivious of conditions below the deck.　（CAt　Shinya Omura）

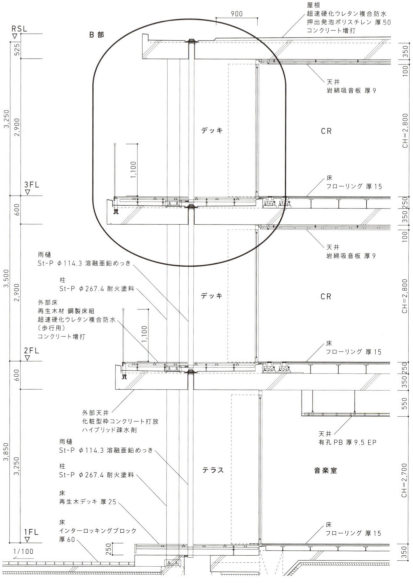

A－A矩計（SECTION A-A）　1／80

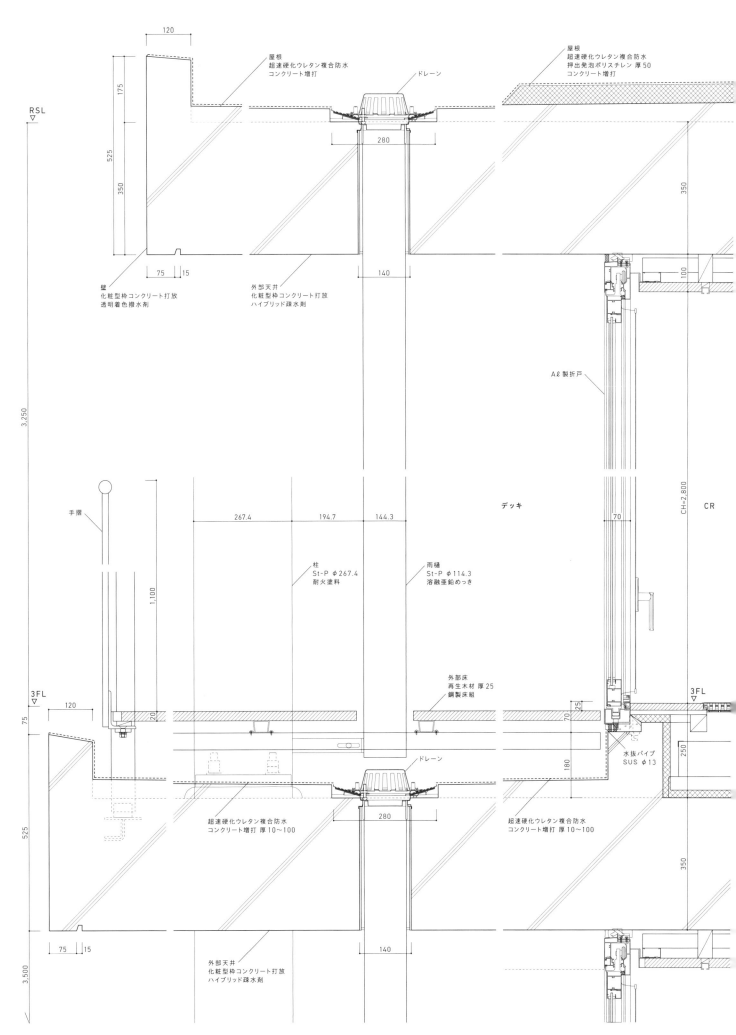

B部断面詳細（DETAILED SECTION B） 1／10

Balcony 17

内外が一体に
感じられる
軒庇

Deck Design for
Interior-Exterior Continuity

大阪木材仲買会館
竹中工務店

Osaka Timber Association Building
Takenaka Corporation

施工：竹中工務店
構造：RC造＋木造
規模：地上3階
竣工：2013年3月
所在：大阪府大阪市
撮影：彰国社写真部（p88），母倉知樹（p89, 90）

Constructor: Takenaka Corporation
Structure: RC+W
Number of stories: 3 stories
Completion date: March, 2013
Location: Osaka-city, Osaka
Photo: Shokokusha Photographer (p88),
Tomoki Hahakura (p89, 90)

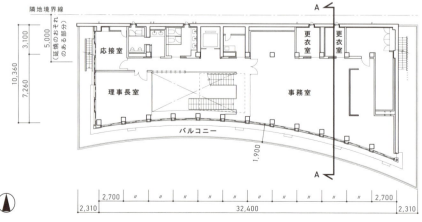

2階平面（2nd FLOOR PLAN）　1／400

大阪木材仲買会館は、耐火木造を用いることで実現した、木材を取り扱う組合の木造オフィスである。外観の大部分に配された木製建具と、それを日差しや雨から保護する目的も兼ねた軒庇でファサードを構成した。防水計画・雨水計画では樋や防水の仕舞がファサード側に表出しない計画を目指した。主屋根の雨水は隣地境界側に片流れ屋根として流し、主屋根下の各層の軒庇は吹き込んだ雨水のみ外構に直接流す計画とした。この軒庇は跳出しバルコニー形状の部分から屋上テラスへと連続している。居室上部の防水性能を確保しつつ、内外が一体的に感じられるサッシとデッキ納まりを高さ方向の寸法を抑えながら実現するにあたって、防水立上りの納まりがシンプルでかつ施工の容易さを考慮して、超速硬化ウレタン複合防水を採用した。

（竹中工務店　白波瀬智幸・興津俊宏）

The osaka timber association building, housing the offices of a lumber association, is the first fireproof wood building in Japan. The exterior facade is composed mainly of wood fittings, and has deep eaves to protect the wood from sunlight and rain. In waterproof and rainwater design planning, we sought to eliminate gutters and flashing on the facade side. Rainwater falling on the main roof follows the roof slope and drains behind the building at its boundary with adjacent land. Rain slanting in on the decks of the facade, meanwhile, falls directly to the ground outside. From its balcony overhang, the third-floor deck continues inward to become a rooftop terrace. While ensuring sufficient waterproofing capability for the upper portion of rooms, we used a multi-component ultra fast curing polyurethane waterproofing membrane system for simplicity and ease of installation of the containment below the deck flooring. The resulting drainage design permitted the deck to be flush with the door sash for interior and exterior continuity.

(Takenaka Corporation Tomoyuki Shirahase, Toshihiro Okitsu)

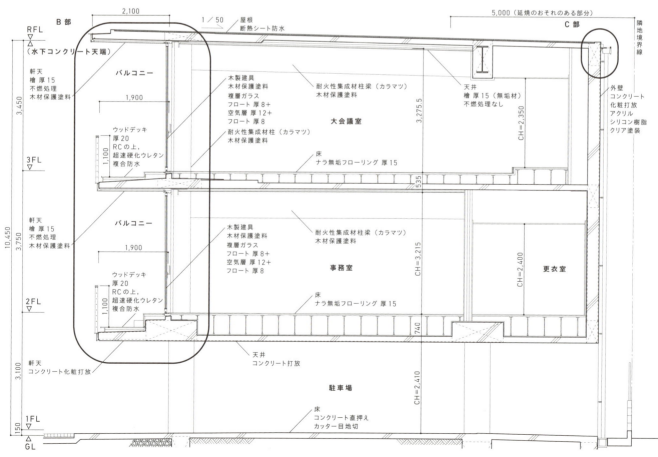

A-A断面（SECTION A-A）　1／100

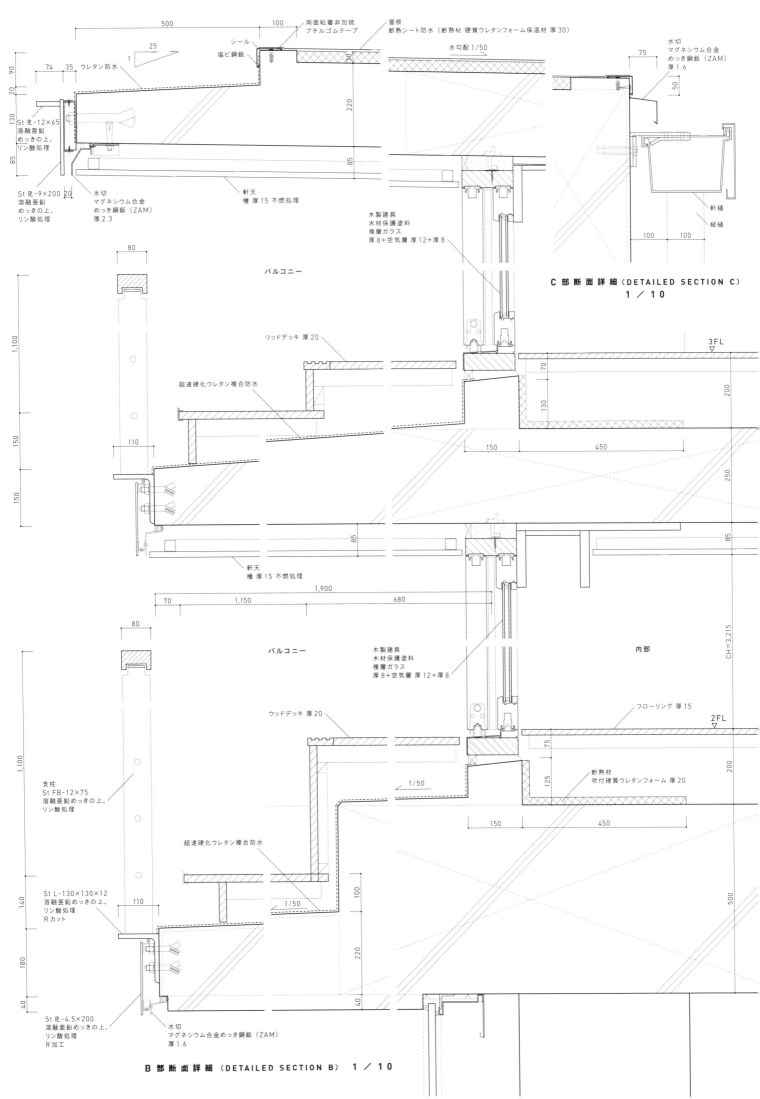

Eaves ## 18

GRC庇を緑化システムで彩る

GRC Eaves Enhanced with Greening System

**関西外国語大学
インターナショナル
コミュニケーションセンター**
日建設計

International Communication Center
Kansai Gaidai University
NIKKEN SEKKEI LTD

施工：竹中工務店
構造：S造，一部SRC造
規模：地上4階，地下1階
竣工：2012年7月
所在：大阪府枚方市
写真提供：日建設計

Constructor: Takenaka Corporation
Structure: S+SRC
Number of stories: 4 stories, 1 basement
Completion date: July, 2012
Location: Hirakata-city, Osaka
Courtesy of: NIKKEN SEKKEI LTD

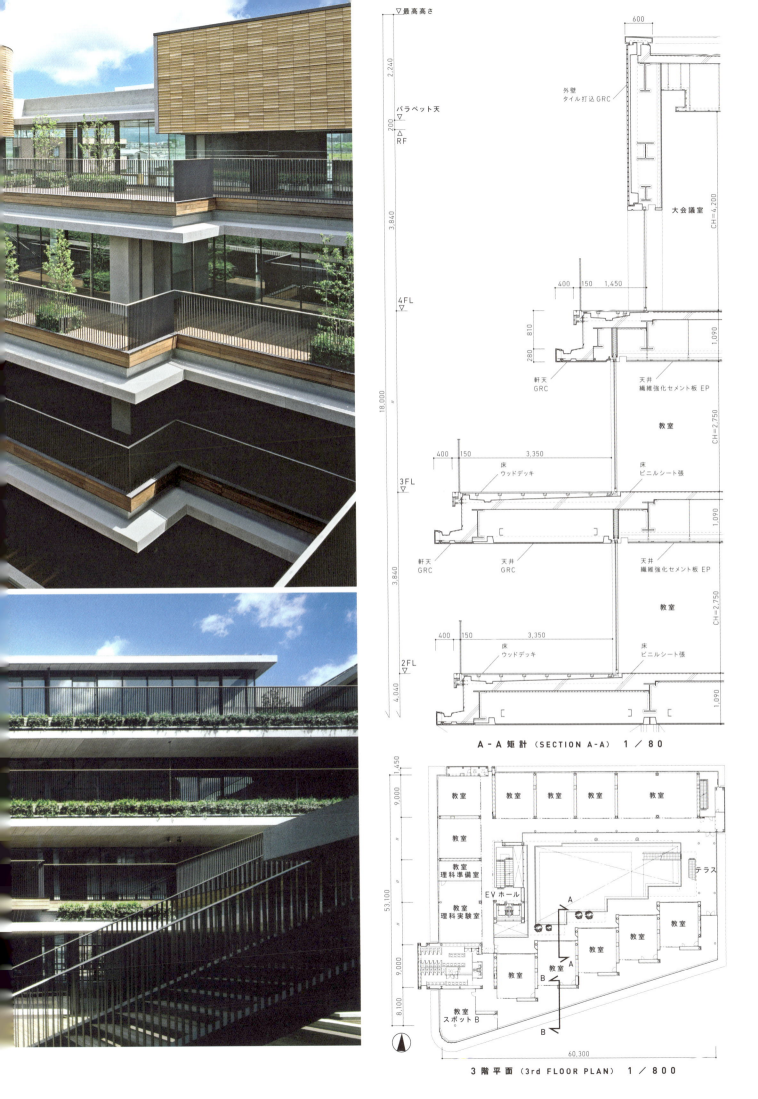

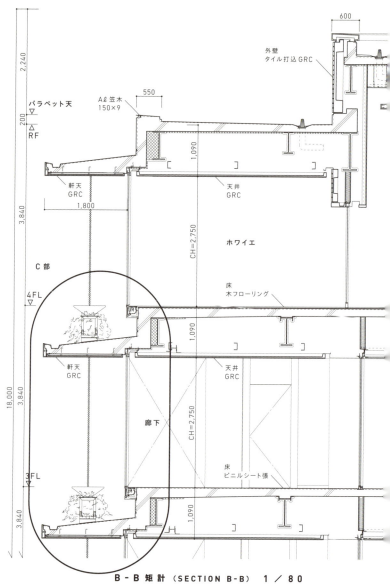

B－B矩計（SECTION B-B） 1／80

学生、地域住民、社会人の知的交流を図ることを目的とし、地域、世界に開かれた新しい教育の創造・創発の場としての施設。深い庇に守られた透明感あるファサードで内部の活気が表通りや中庭にあふれ出す計画とし、地域住民参加イベントなどの先駆的な取組みや活動を広く街や社会にアピールする、ショーケースとしてのデザインを志向した。
共用部天井は豆砂利を仕込み特殊工法で鏡面仕上げとしたGRCとし、2辺支持ガラスを通して内外連続で展開。周囲の緑や通りの賑わい、学生の動きなどが庇を介して柔らかく天井に映し込まれ、緑豊かな中庭・外部空間との一体感を感じる光にあふれた快適な学習空間を実現した。特徴あるファサードの庇に組み込む緑化システムとして立体緑化プランターを採用。レール架台をスラブに固定し、緑化システムを設置している。金物の多い庇上面に防水を施すため、施工性のよい緑化における耐バクテリア仕様の超速硬化ウレタン複合防水を採用した。この防水がなければ実現が難しいディテールである。（日建設計　多喜茂）

The facility is a place for the creation and emergence of new education, opened up to the local community and the world, with the aim of promoting intellectual exchange among student, local residents and other visitors. The building has been designed as a showcase in order to widely promote pioneering initiatives and activities, such as local resident participation events, within the local and wider communities, with the plan that the inner vitality of the school will spill out into the main street and courtyard, with the transparency of the facade protected by deep eaves. The ceiling portion of the common space features GRC with inlaid pea gravel specially treated to give a mirror finish, and the interior and exterior extend continuously through 2-sided support glass. The surrounding greenery, the vitality of the streets and the activity of the students are all reflected softly onto the ceiling through the eaves, realizing a pleasant learning space that is filled with a light that brings a sense of unity between the lush greenery of the courtyard and the external spaces. Greening planters have been used in a greening system that is built into the eaves of the characteristic facade. Rail mounts are fixed to the slabs, with the greening system installed. In order to provide waterproofing for the upper surface of the eaves, which feature many metal fixtures, superfast hardening multi-component ultra fast curing polyurethane waterproofing membrane system has been used for its antibacterial properties in good workability greening. Without it, this detail would have been difficult to achieve. (NIKKEN SEKKEI LTD Shigeru Taki)

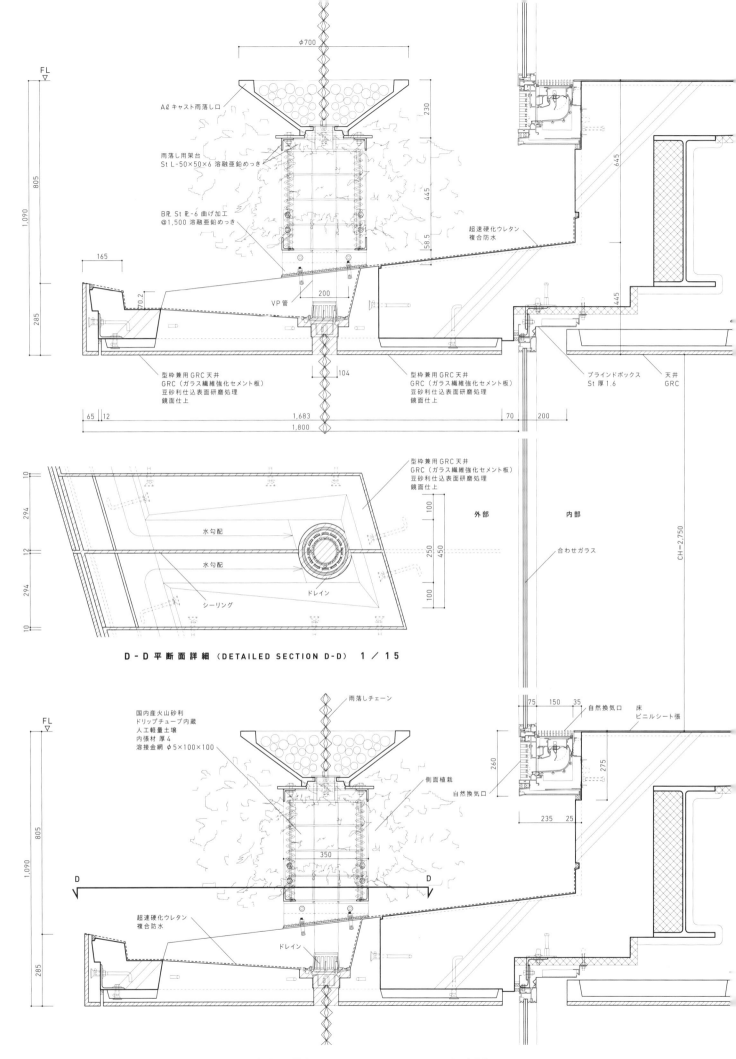

D-D平断面詳細 (DETAILED SECTION D-D) 1/15

C部断面詳細 (DETAILED SECTION C) 1/15

Eaves 19

「裳階」に倣ったPC版と鉄板の二重庇

Double Eaves of PC Units and Iron Plates Resembling a "Mokoshi"

**独立行政法人国立文化財機構
奈良文化財研究所**
日本設計

Nara National Research Institute
for Cultural Properties
National Institutes for Cultural Heritage
NIHON SEKKEI, INC.

施工：鴻池組
構造：SRC造・S造
規模：地上4階，地下2階
竣工：2018年3月
所在：奈良県奈良市
撮影：稲住泰広

Constructor: KONOIKE CONSTRUCTION CO.,LTD.
Structure: SRC+S
Number of stories: 4 stories, 2 basements
Completion date: March, 2018
Location: Nara-city, Nara
Photo: Yasuhiro Inazumi

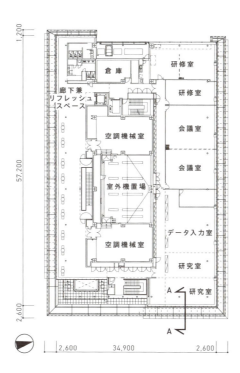
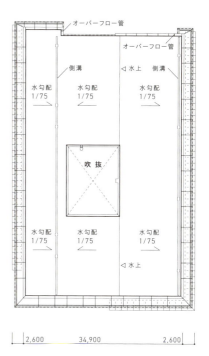

4階平面（4th FLOOR PLAN）
1／800

屋根伏（ROOF PLAN）
1／800

DETAIL extra issue 97

敷地は、平城宮の西面中門である佐伯門の西に位置し、発掘調査により平城京の東西の幹線道路である一条南大路とその側溝、西一坊大路や秋篠川旧流路などの遺構の残存が判明した場所である。計画・設計に際しては、この遺構の保存を最優先とすることが求められた。遺構保存範囲を避けて建物を配置しながら、奈良時代の大路のスケールを感じられるランドスケープとしている。建築には、風致地区条例による絶対高さ15m以下や外装・屋根の色・素材等の制限もあった。必要とされるヴォリュームを確保するために、地上部では片持ち形状で建設可能範囲よりも大きく張り出す構造計画・平面計画を行い、そして階高を3.55mに抑え、地上部に4層の空間を設けた。屋根防水に超速硬化ウレタン複合防水を採用し、納まりを簡素化することも、その制限をクリアすることの一つとして寄与している。階高を抑え、楼閣建築の「裳階」に倣ったL形PC版と鉄板の二重庇による低く深い軒が印象的な水平線と陰影を生み、奈良の地に静かに佇む建築が完成した。

（日本設計　東本光尚（元所員））

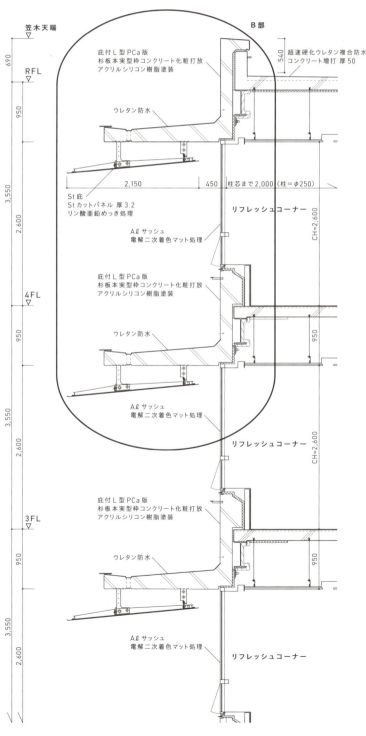

A－A矩計（SECTION A-A）　1／60

The site is just west of Saekimon Gate, the central gate on the west side of Heijo Palace. Excavations at the site have revealed remnants of Southern First Avenue—the main east-west thoroughfare through the Heijo capital—and the avenue's gutter, as well as West First Avenue and the ancient Akishino River watercourse. We were required to give priority to preserving these remnants in the project's planning and design. While locating the building to avoid the remnants, we created a landscape evoking the grand scale of the Nara Period. The architecture was subject to scenic zone regulations concerning colors and materials used on the roof and exterior, and could not be higher than an absolute 15m. In order to secure the necessary volume, we undertook structural and plan design to extend the building beyond the limits of the construction site in the form of a cantilever above the ground. Restraining the floor height to 3.55m, we established four floors above ground. The use of a multi-component ultra fast curing polyurethane waterproofing membrane system on the roof simplified the waterproofing details and contributed to clearing the scenic zone restrictions. Restraining the floor height, we used L-shaped precast concrete units and iron plates to establish double eaves resembling the "mokoshi" pent roof used in traditional buildings. The low, deep eaves produce distinctive horizontal lines and shadows in a building standing quietly, in harmony with Nara's ancient past. (NIHON SEKKEI, INC. Mitsuhisa Higashimoto (Former Staff))

B部断面詳細 (DETAILED SECTION B) 1／15

Eaves

20

PCa版による大庇の積層表現

PCa Slabs to Achieve a Large-eaved Layered Expression

新ダイビル
日建設計

Shin-Daibiru Building
NIKKEN SEKKEI LTD

施工：大林組
PCa版工事：マキテック，高橋カーテンウォール
カーテンウォール工事：YKK AP
構造：S造，SRC造，RC造
規模：地上31階，地下2階，塔屋3階
竣工：2015年3月
所在：大阪府大阪市
撮影：彰国社写真部（p100, 101），木原慎二（p102）

Constructor: OBAYASHI CORPORATION
PCa panel work : Makitech Japan Corporation,
TAKAHASHI CURTAIN WALL CORPORATION
Curtain wall work : YKK AP
Structure: S+SRC+RC
Number of stories: 31 stories, 2 basements,
3 penthouse stories
Completion date: March, 2015
Location: Osaka-city, Osaka
Photo: Shokokusha Photographer（p100, 101），
Shinji Kihara（p102）

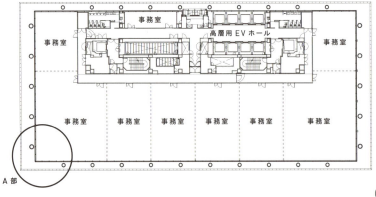

基準階平面（TIPICAL FLOOR PLAN） 1／800

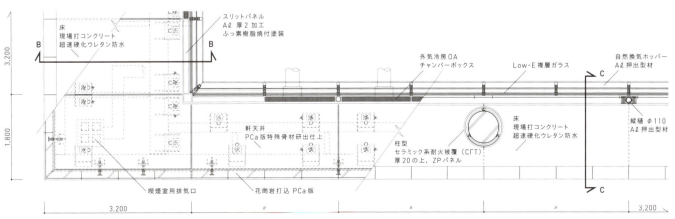

A部平面（PLAN A） 1／80

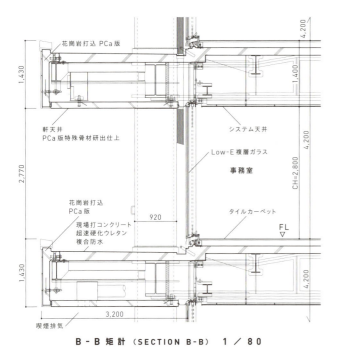

B－B矩計（SECTION B-B） 1／80

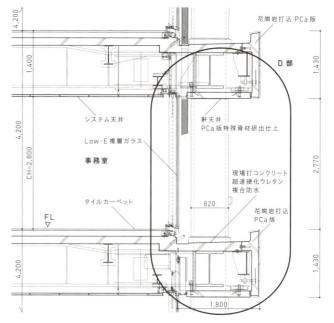

C－C矩計（SECTION C-C） 1／80

中之島を一望する抜群の眺望と、先代ビルの屋上樹苑を継承した大規模緑地を生かすことが設計のテーマであった。ブラインドなしで眺望を享受できるよう、日射角に応じ東西3.2m南北1.8mの大庇を設置。天井懐とほぼ同じ1.4mの厚みをもたせ「積層するスラブ」というシンプルな形式に還元し、遮るものなく「緑と眺望」を楽しめる外装を目指した。

外周柱はアウトフレームとして、すべてバルコニー側に配置。室内に一切の柱形が現れない整形無柱空間とし、フレキシビリティを高めている。オフィスから見えるこのバルコニーの床は、仕上げを兼ねたトップコートにマット仕上げを施しギラギラ感を抑えた超速硬化ウレタン複合防水を採用し、意匠性に配慮したバルコニーを実現している。

（日建設計　多喜茂）

The design theme was to take advantage of the outstanding vista overlooking Nakanoshima and make the best use of the large green space inherited from the rooftop gardens of the earlier building. In order to be able to enjoy the views without the obstruction of blinds, large eaves were installed at 3.2m Northeast and 1.8m Southwest, in accordance with the solar radiation angle. Reducing the design to the simple form of "layered slabs" of a thickness of 1.4m, almost the same as the ceiling cavity, the aim was to create an exterior that allows users of the building to enjoy "the greenery and the view" without obstruction.

The outer columns are arranged on the balcony side, as out frames. The interior is a column-free space that offers increased flexibility. The floor of the balcony, viewable from the offices, is finished with a multi-component ultra fast curing polyurethane waterproofing membrane system layer that doubles as a matte finish top coat that cuts down glare and gives the balcony a strong sense of design consciousness. （NIKKEN SEKKEI LTD　Shigeru Taki）

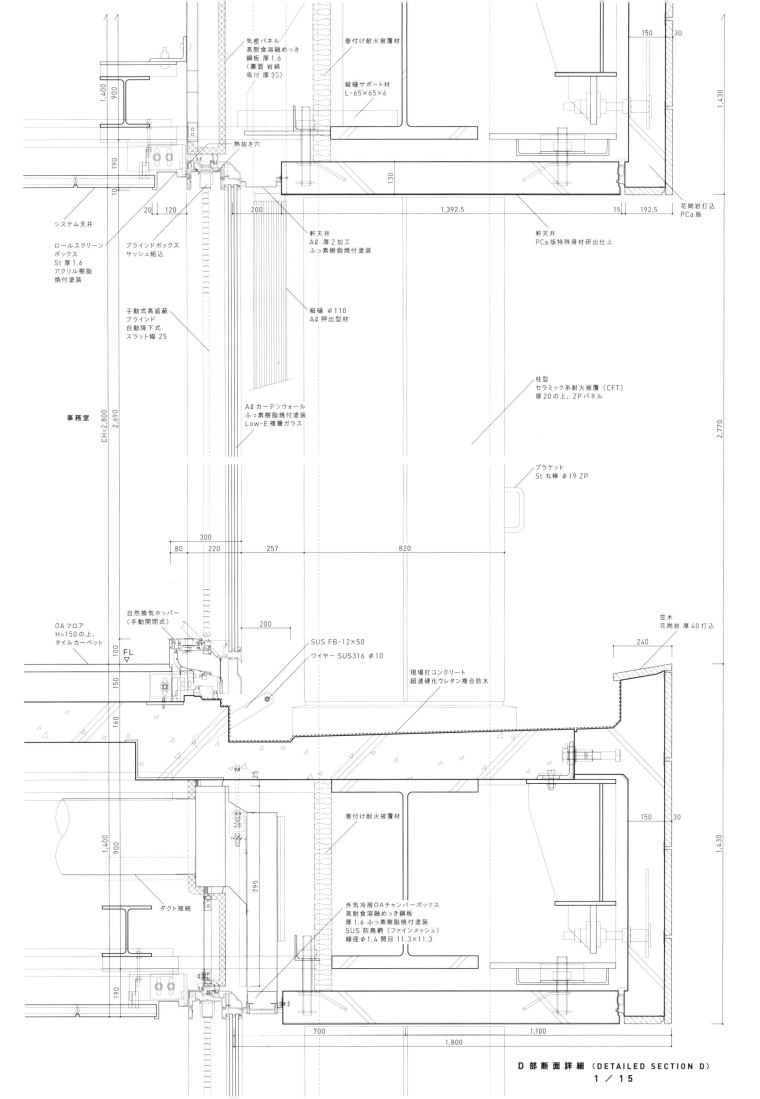

D部断面詳細 (DETAILED SECTION D)
1／15

Project 21

鉄骨・RC・木造の超速硬化ウレタン複合防水

Multi-component Ultra Fast Curing Polyurethane Waterproofing Membrane for Steel Frame, RC, and Wood Structures

追手門学院大学 新キャンパス
三菱地所設計

Otemon Gakuin University New Campus
MITSUBISHI JISHO SEKKEI INC.

施工：竹中工務店
構造：大学棟／S+SRC造，食堂棟／RC造+S造，バス停／RC造，一部木造
規模：大学棟／地上5階 食堂棟，バス停／地上1階
竣工：2019年3月
所在：大阪府茨木市
撮影：西川公朗（p104-105, 107），
黒住直臣（p106, 108, 110）

Constructor: Takenaka Corporation
Structure: College Building／S+SRC,
Cafeteria Building／RC+S, Bus Station／RC+W
Number of stories: College Building／5 stories,
Cafeteria Building, Bus Station／1 story
Completion date: March, 2019
Location: Ibaraki-city, Osaka
Photo: Masao Nishikawa (p104-105, 107),
Naoomi Kurozumi (p106, 108, 110)

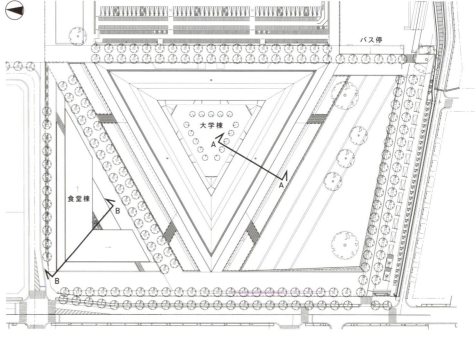

配置（SITE PLAN） 1／2,000

大学棟"Omusubi"は図書館を中心に周囲に教室を配した平面形状であり、断面も図書館が宙に浮き地上階を大きな多目的エリアとしたメイン棟である。"おむすび"形は構造的にも強く、厚1.2mの構造壁12個で一辺約130mの三角形を持ち上げている。三角形の先端はエントランスとし、約40mのキャンティレバーが人々を迎え入れると同時に、1階の多目的ホールとともに有事の際に地域の防災拠点として利用できる工夫もしている。

キャスト建築として、新たに桜の花びらをステンレスキャストのみでパネル化した外装となっている。これは桜模様のアルミ鋳造でつくった「追手門学院大学1号館」(20頁)、さらに台湾を象徴する花である梅をモチーフに、アルミでなくステンレスチューブ加工とステンレスキャストの複合パネルで覆った「臺北南山廣場」商業棟(44頁)で培ったノウハウを生かした。外装と防水の断面詳細はどの事例もほぼ同じである。屋根面、鉄やステンレスの取付け金物、躯体を超速硬化ウレタン複合防水で一面に覆い防水できるクイックスプレー工法でしかできない納まりである。

中庭も集中豪雨などを配慮し、多くのドレーンを設けた。また、5mのPCキャンティレバーでつくった大庇により中庭に面したサッシはシンプルな納まりとなっている。(三菱地所設計 須部恭浩)

In plan, the main volume, "Omusubi," features a central library encompassed by classrooms. In section, the library floats in suspension, and the upper floors contain a large multipurpose area. The "Omusubi" (triangular rice ball) shape is structurally sturdy. Twelve 1.2m-thick structural walls support a triangle some 130m to a side. The entrances are at the points of the triangle, where a 40m cantilever greets visitors. In emergencies, the entrances and multipurpose hall on the first floor can perform as a regional disaster center. Giving play to knowhow gained in creating "Otemon Gakuin 1st Building (page 20)" clad in cast aluminum cherry blossoms, and the "Taipei Nan Shan Plaza (page 44)" commercial facility clad in plum blossoms (Taiwan's national flower) made not of aluminum but composite panels of shaped stainless steel pipe and cast stainless steel, we returned to cherry blossom-motif cladding, this time in panels using only cast stainless steel. In section, the detailing of the exterior wall and waterproofing is nearly the same in each case, it being an assembly only possible using the Quick Spray method of applying multi-component ultra fast curing polyurethane waterproofing membrane system over the roof surface, iron and stainless steel attachments, and building frame. In the open court, numerous drains were installed for response to torrential rains. The use of large, cantilevered 5-meter precast-concrete eaves, moreover, enabled a simple assembly for the sashes fronting on the court. (MITSUBISHI JISHO SEKKEI INC., Yasuhiro Sube)

大学棟「Omusubi」｜脱気口なしのシームレスな屋上防水と屋上緑化
'Omusubi' College Building｜Minimal and Seamless Waterproofing and Greening

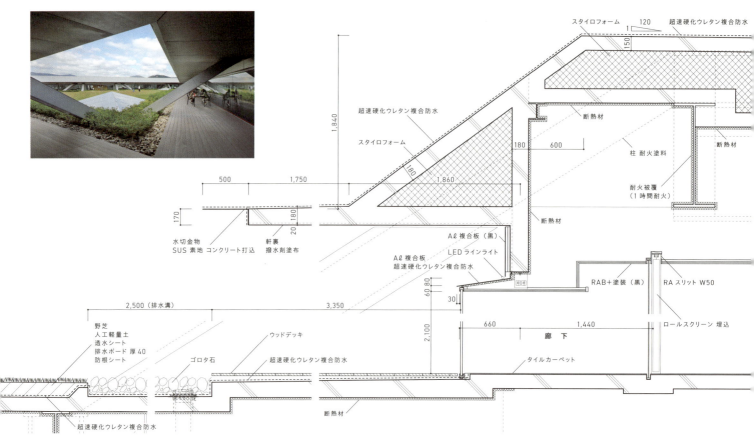

C部断面詳細 (DETAILED SECTION C) 1/40

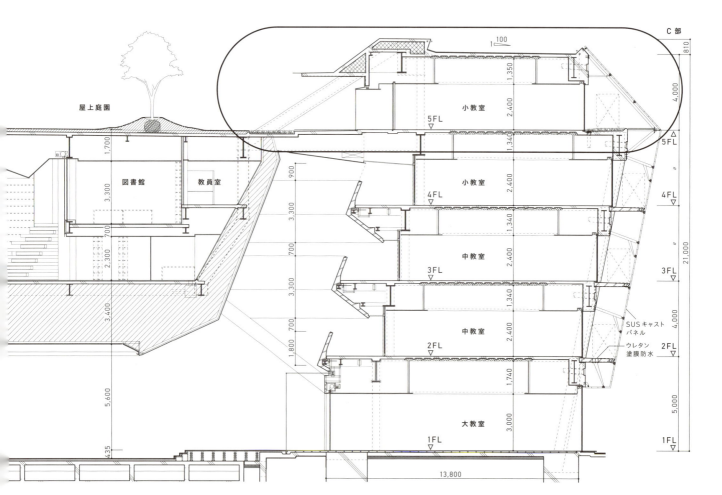

A-A断面 (SECTION A-A) 1/200

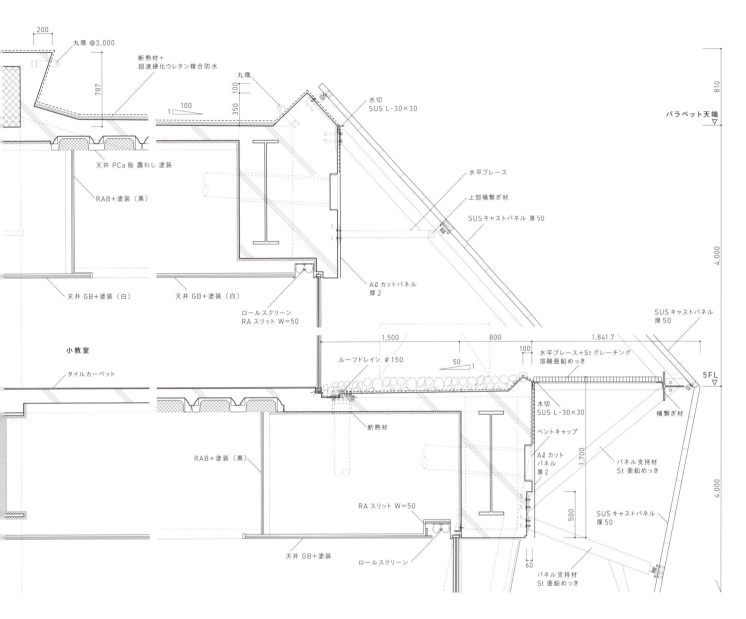

食堂棟｜RC屋根を"見せる防水"
Cafeteria Building｜"Displayable Waterproofing" for an RC Roof

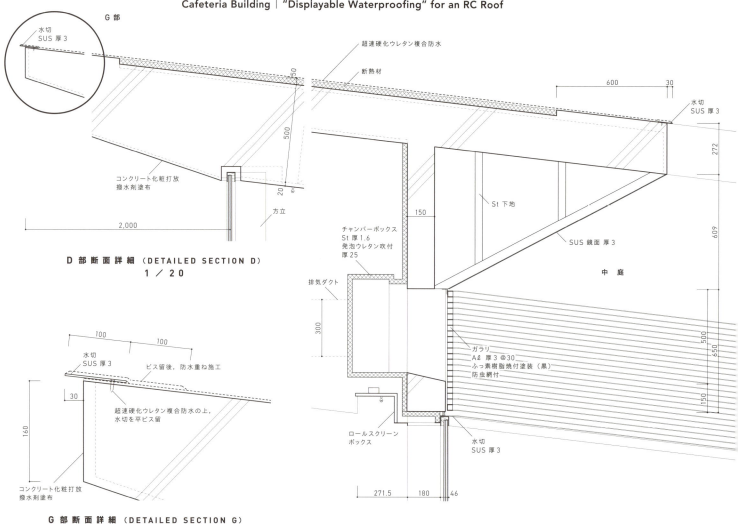

D部断面詳細（DETAILED SECTION D）1／20

G部断面詳細（DETAILED SECTION G）1／6

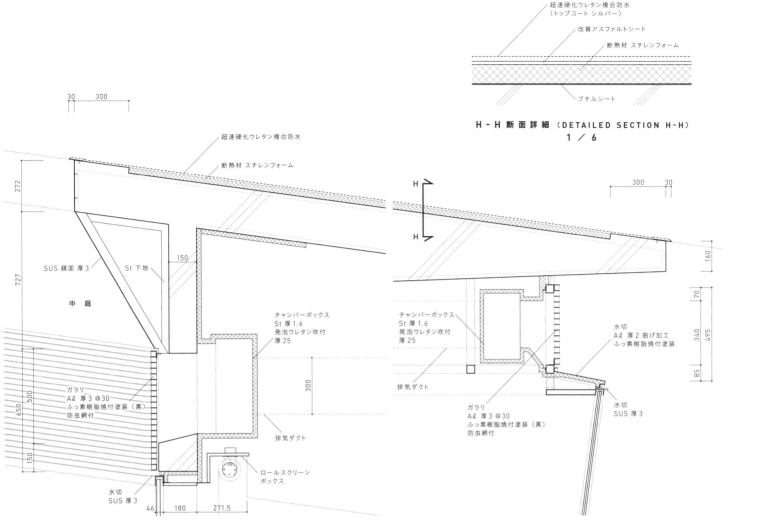

2枚のコンクリートが貝のように交差点に向かい口を開いた「く」の字形の断面が特徴の、街に開く学生食堂である。大学棟とは運営時間、利用形態も違うため別棟とした。コストを抑え大空間をつくるためコンクリート2枚のうち1枚を床、もう1枚を屋根とし、「く」の字の板の交差部に耐力壁を設けた。

厨房となる部分は低く、交差点に面した街に賑わいを見せる部分を高くしている。一面に脱気口がない超速硬化ウレタン複合防水の進化形を開発することで、シンプルな1枚の大きな板のコンクリートの屋根をつくることができた。バス停（110頁）と同じく落ち葉が多い場所のため、ドレーンは設けず、犬走りに雨水を落とすだけのディテールである。屋根のRC板の水切りは、SUS厚3mmを小口面より30mm出すことで壁面の汚れを防ぐことができる。（三菱地所設計　須部恭浩）

This volume, a student cafeteria open to the city, is distinguished by two concrete slabs opening clam-like towards the intersection, forming a great "V" in section. The cafeteria is housed in a separate volume because it differs in operating hours and manner of usage from the main building. To restrain costs and engender a large space, one of the two concrete slabs is a floor and the other a roof, with a load-bearing wall established at the intersection of the two slabs.

With the kitchen in the low portion, the cafeteria occupies the high space fronting on the intersection, displaying its activities to the city. By developing an evolved version of multi-component ultra fast curing polyurethane waterproofing membrane system having no deaeration ports, we could create a concrete roof from a simple large concrete slab. Like the bus stop (page 110), the site has many fallen leaves, so rainwater is simply fed into a berm without the use of a drain. By extending the 3mm-thick drainage board of the roof's RC slab 30mm beyond the transverse section, we could prevent rainwater from befouling the wall.

（MITSUBISHI JISHO SEKKEI INC.,　Yasuhiro Sube）

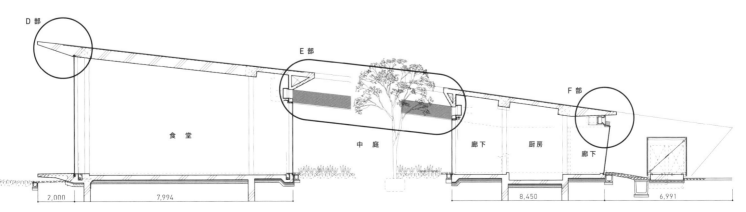

バス停｜大判CLT集成材のフラット屋根の防水
Bus Station | Waterproofing a Large-size CLT Flat Roof

RC壁柱に3m×30m程度の大判CLT集成材を載せたシンプルなバス停である。素材を選ばずシームレスに一体成形できる超速硬化ウレタン複合防水のメリットを生かし、30分耐火認定の木とボードの複合認定を用いたフラット屋根とした。経験上、水切りはSUS厚3mmを小口面より30mm出すことで壁面の汚れを防ぐことができる。笠木がなく、パラペットもなくコストも抑えられる。また、高木などが多く落ち葉が多い場所ではドレーンが詰まるため、ドレーンを設けず犬走りに雨を落とす納まりである。屋根面のメンテナンスをする必要もなく、コストとメンテナンスの両面で有効なディテールである。（三菱地所設計　須部恭浩）

A simple bus station composed only of an RC wall-column capped with large-size 3mx30m cross-laminated timber (CLT). Giving play to capability of multi-component ultra fast curing polyurethane waterproofing membrane system to form an overall seamless membrane, regardless of materials involved, we created a flat roof using a compound of 30-minute fire retardant wood and board. From experience, by extending the 3mm-thick drainage board of the roof's RC slab 30mm beyond the transverse section, we could prevent rainwater from befouling the wall. Eliminating a coping and parapet helped restrain costs. Then, because of fallen leaves from many tall trees, a drain would clog, so rainwater is simply fed into a berm without the use of a drain. The completed roof surface is an attractive detail low in cost and maintenance. (MITSUBISHI JISHO SEKKEI INC., Yasuhiro Sube)

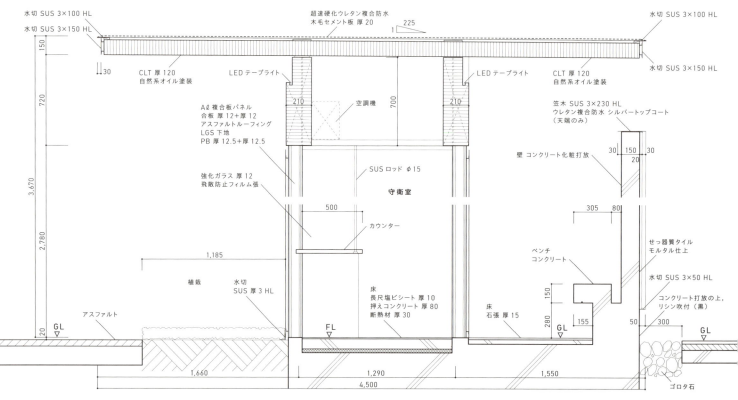

断面詳細 (DETAILED SECTION) 1／30

超速硬化ウレタン複合防水が建築デザインを変える

Round Table
Multi-component Ultra Fast Curing
Polyurethane Waterproofing
Membrane Systems
Will Change Architectural Design

鼎談

赤松佳珠子（CAt）
Kazuko AKAMATSU

須部恭浩（三菱地所設計）
Yasuhiro SUBE

多喜茂（日建設計）
Shigeru TAKI

溜めるディテールから、溢れさせるディテールへ

須部 ここ数年、建築の本防水として超速硬化ウレタン防水が使われるようになりつつあります。

振り返ると、バブルがはじけた後の2000年ごろに一つの転換期があったように思います。当時は予算も限られて無駄をできるだけなくすことが求められるなかで、笠木などが不要で省施工、なおかつ工期も短い超速硬化ウレタン防水は設計者に魅力的に映ったのだと思います。私の場合は、当初ゼネコンの担当者が技術研究所に持ち込んで性能を確認してくれるなど、バックアップ体制があったのも大きい。

多喜 当時のウレタン防水というと、おそらく多くの人は屋上のハト小屋やパラペットの上に塗ってあるものという認識で、ぺらぺらの薄い膜の防水という程度のイメージしかなかったのではないでしょうか。当時、信頼性はアスファルト防水にありましたから。

赤松 たとえばアスファルト防水の屋上だと、パラペットの立上りを取ってアゴを設けて、コンクリートで押さえてと、どんどんディテールが複雑になっていきます。でも、超速硬化ウレタン防水は基本的にはすごくシンプルな納まりで済む。私たちの事務所の場合は、スタッフがそうした超速硬化ウレタン防水の情報や事例を集めてきて、性能、コスト、そして意匠上の納まりなどを総合的に判断して使ってみたのが最初です。

須部 赤松さんがいま「シンプルになる」とおっしゃいましたが、まさにその点が大きいと思います。

私たちが教わった防水のディテールは複雑で、防水層の上に押えコンクリートがあって、理由ははっきりしないのですがパラペットの立上りは600mm以上取りなさいと神話のように教わりました。パラペットにはアゴをつくって、乾式のボードや湿式の保護材で保護する。そして、あるピッチでオーバーフロー管を設けて、水を溜めてオーバーフローさせる。ただ、これだけ複雑になると施工上管理もしにくいし、さらに経年劣化とともにそうしたものが何かしらの不具合を起こすわけです（fig.1）。

古くは、日本の家屋には犬走りがあって、屋根の水は垂れたその下できちんと対応していました。いわば、水を屋根から溢れさせることを考えたディテールです。そのほうが部屋の中にいる人にとっては安全・安心なのですよね。そういったディテールが、ほぼ勾配のない陸屋根でも超速硬化ウレタン防水によって可能になったというのが、設計者が採用し始めた理由の一つでもあるのかなと思います（fig.2）。

想定外をイメージした納まりが可能に

多喜 FRP防水一つとっても、私たちが入社した当時でも信頼性はそれなりに高かったけれども、15年くらいで笠木の際が浮いてくることもあり、そこから防水層に水が入り出すとどこに回ったかわからない。一方、超速硬化ウレタン防水は、液剤を専用の機械で吹き付けて直接コンクリートなどの面に付着させるので、仕上がりは密着した状態です。緊急時に、極論すれば池になってもいい。立上りのある陸屋根などでも水が外に溢れるときに漏水しなければ建物は水から守られますね。

いま想定外といわれる集中豪雨の問題がありますけど、オーバーフロー管のディテールには想定の範囲がありますよね。先ほど須部さんが溢れさせるディテールと言ったように、超速硬化ウレタン複合防水の納まりは、妙な言い方ですが、想定外のときのイメージができるというのが、いまの時代に合っているのかなと思います。もちろん、階段の開口や入口のレベルよりも先に外へ水がきちんと流れるという、根本的なレベル関係をつくっておくことは必須ですが。

須部 従来は完璧につくったところにわざわざ後からオーバーフローのための穴を開けていました。ディテールの点から見てもそれよりは確実に安全です。コンクリートだから、金属だからという素材の違いも関係なく密着しますし、パラペットのアゴを最後につくらなくてもいい。

結果的に、従来のパラペット分の600mmが、たとえば100mmや50mmになることで、その分、各階の人が過ごす空間に振り分けることができる。これも私たち設計者が望んでいたことなんじゃないかと思います。

赤松 公共の学校建築の場合、全体のコストを抑えるために、階高を抑えながらいかに中の空間を高く取るかが設計において重要です。そのときに、パラペットの立上りが少なくて済むというのは理

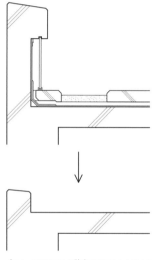

fig.1 アスファルト防水のパラペット（上）と超速硬化ウレタン防水のパラペット（下）

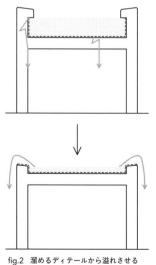

fig.2 溜めるディテールから溢れさせるディテールへ

にかなっていますし、コストメリットも大きい。フットプリントの大きい建築の場合、コンクリート量の削減量は結構なものになりますから。

これまでは順番に重ねていかなければいけなかったものが必要なくなれば、欠点になるところも少なくなっていくといえます。

須部 押えコンクリートをしないことで地震時の荷重条件もまったく違いますよね。杭が小さくなり、柱が細くなり、梁が小さくなる……。それにより構造的にもVE（Value Engineering）になり、安全性や空間にプラスになる。地震国日本においては大事なことだと思います。

須部恭浩（すべやすひろ）

仕組みがシンプルだからこそ、問題解決も早い

多喜 私が入社したころはウレタン防水もゴムアスファルトとの複合防水が主流でした。ステンレス防水、FRP防水、シート防水、アスファルト防水といったものがありますが、いずれにしても「膜」を張って防水するものですから、防水層に隙間が生じます。ということは、どこか1カ所から裏に水がまわった途端に、どこから出るかわからないうえ、出るまでのタイムラグが発生するということです。

一方、現在の超速硬化ウレタン複合防水は、コンクリート面など施工面に完全にひっついてしまうので、基本的には補修すべきところが見つかったら、他のところは密着しているので水がまわらず、その部分だけを補修すればいいわけです。仕組みがとてもシンプルだから、万が一水が漏れたとしても、原因究明も早い。私にとってはそこが従来とは考え方が飛躍的に違う防水だと思いますし、それが一番のポイントだと思っています。逆にいえば、防水面より躯体の状態のほうが気になります。特に防水を施工するコンクリート表面の状態とか、レイタンスを取り除いた状態がベストですね。

須部 防水メーカーなどの10年保証がありますから、それらは管理者にとっても施主にとっても施工者にとっても安心です。施主側としても一定期間の保証をしてくれて、空間も広くなるなら採用しようという一つの根拠になります。

では10年後の防水はどうなっているのかと考えると、いまの改修の状況を見ていると、ウレタン防水が他の防水に取って代わっていくのではないかと思います。

多喜 現在の改修事例の多くでは、既存のアスファルト防水の押えコンクリートの上から超速硬化ウレタン複合防水を塗っていますものね。

須部 そうすると、いまの時点で10年間は本防水がアスファルト防水だといっても、改修工事をした途端に、それ以降のかなり長い期間の防水はウレタン防水に変わるという非合理的なことになってしまう。

さらにアスファルト防水だと熱が必要で、臭いの問題、火事の危険性などがありますが、それらの問題が超速硬化ウレタン防水にはありませんから施工者も安全で、協力体制をつくってもらいやすい。

経済的な状況や施工のこと、設計者の要望も満足すること、改修事例が増えていくタイミングであったことなど、いろいろな要因が働いたのが2000年以後の状況なのかなと思います。

超速硬化ウレタン複合防水のディテール

赤松 設計の視点で見ると、最も大きな違いはモノとモノの取合いですね。

たとえばアスファルト防水では、一般に取合いの端部から水が入って雨漏りするというのが多いと思います。絶対に大丈夫だと言われて採用したステンレスのシームレス溶接の防水も、経年による金属疲労でクラックが入ってしまったときは衝撃を受けました。一方、超速硬化ウレタン防水は端部でもぴったりと密着しているから、防水層に水が入らない。

須部 僕らが若いころ雑誌で見ていた、工夫されたいわゆるきわどい納まりのときには、わりとシート防水が使われていたように思います。

追手門学院大学（設計：三菱地所設計）
撮影：黒住直臣

DETAIL extra issue 113

赤松　シート防水でも、立上りの入隅はどうしても弱点になりやすいですよね。

須部　超速硬化ウレタン複合防水は、物ではなく液体で現場に届いて、それを吹き付けるという発想で、FRPのお風呂のような継目がないシームレスなものが巨大な空間でできてしまう。そういう意味では、これまでとはまったく違う考え方ですね。

赤松　超速硬化ウレタン複合防水で下には水が入らないという意味では安心ですけれど、あとはサッシュの下端とか、要は部材の取合いですよね。いまの話では防水層というよりは、サッシュのシールから水がまわるとか、そういうことになっていく。

赤松佳珠子（あかまつかずこ）

須部　そういう点では、今回事例がまとめて紹介される意味がありますよね。

　私の場合は、サッシュの手前にステンレスなどの金物を設けて、水が中へ入り込まないようにしたうえで、サッシュの後ろの室内側に立上りを取って、そこまで防水を巻き上げています。外部はウッドデッキなど乾式のものを置いて、室内のOAフロアなどでフラットにするというディテールをよく使います（fig.3）。

多喜　みんなそれぞれ工夫して、最低限これというルールをみんなそれぞれもっているんですね。私はシールが切れても水上にじわじわと水が入ってほしくないものですから、サッシュ下のシールのところで必ず2cmくらいは立ち上げています。加えて勾配は、ウレタン防水でも1/50にと言っています（fig.4）。

須部　1/100以下の勾配ではダメという、そうした数値もありますね。

赤松　基本的には、水は溜めてはいけないというのがベースにあると思います。砂埃や落ち葉といったものが水を含んでしまうと、1/100ですと、場所によっては水が流れていかず、水たまりができてしまう。上から見えるようなところではきれいなものではないですから、ある程度水が流れる勾配にしています。仮にドレーンのところでゴミが溜まっても、そこを掃除すればいい。何かが起こっても、最低限目に見えるところで処理できるようには考えています。

設計者・施工者がさらに使いやすいものへ

多喜　超速硬化ウレタン複合防水が登場してまだ十数年だと思いますが、ディテールが単純になりシンプルに建築をつくれるようになった反面、防水自体の意匠性には改良の余地はまだありますよね。表面に施すトップコートの質感も、いまは艶がありますが、たとえばモルタルやコンクリートのようなマットな質感になったらいいのにと思うことはよくあります。

須部　モルタル防水が使われているのをたまに目にしますが、あの質感は確かに魅力的ですね。補修材には含浸させるものがあるけれど、そういう感覚のものが超速硬化ウレタン防水でもできたら面白いのかもしれません。

　それと、私が特に感じているのは、どうやって施工ミスをなくすかということです。たとえば、アスファルト防水は色が黒ですから、施工しているか、していないかは一目瞭然です。でも、超速硬化ウレタン防水の吹付け作業は当然人が行うので、「ここは吹き付けただろう」と思い込んでしまうことが一番怖い。

　それを防ぐためにも、たとえば下地のコンクリート等とはまったく違う色にすれば、吹き付けていない部分が一目でわかりますし、時間が経つと色が変化して同化するようなものであれば、なおさら使いやすくなります。

多喜　人ということでいえば、扱う人への教育や学習の問題もありますね。これ

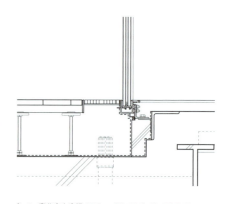

fig.3　臺北南山廣場（設計：三菱地所設計、瀚亞國際設計）商業棟のテラス部分（1/20）

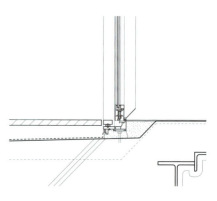

fig.4　関西外国語大学インターナショナルコミュニケーションセンター（設計：日建設計）中庭側のテラス部分（1/20）

流山市立おおたかの森小・中学校（設計：小嶋一浩＋赤松佳珠子／CAt）写真提供：CAt

までは施工事例がそれほど多くなかったので、私たちも現場の人もきちんと勉強しながら施工してきたわけです。でも、広く普及してこれは安全・安心なものだからとなると、そのことだけが一人歩きしだしかねない。施工するにあたって何が大事か、その前提条件が抜け落ちてしまうことがないか少し心配です。

赤松 金属とコンクリートなど、異なる素材では熱の影響も異なり、特に金属は膨張や伸縮もありますから、そういうところでの付着力の変化なども気になるところですね。

須部 塗膜層がどの程度密着しているのか、素材や置かれている環境での違いはどうなのか、そうした数値が具体的なデータとして今後きちんと示されていくといいですね。

多喜 同時に、これからの時代はゼロからすべてを直す時代ではないとすると、たとえば日当りのよい場所と日があまり当たらない場所というように、その場所に合わせた施工後のメンテナンス方法もしだいに見えてくるのではないかと思います。

関西外国語大学インターナショナルコミュニケーションセンター（設計：日建設計）写真提供：日建設計

超速硬化ウレタン複合防水の未来

多喜 超速硬化ウレタンで防水性能が確実に得られるとなったら、その次の段階としては、耐火性能の必要な外壁など、建物全体を覆う場合に、いままでにない性能が防水に求められるでしょうね。

実際にいま直面している課題としては断熱です。室内をコンクリート打放しにしようとすると外断熱になりますが、その上にウレタン防水をどんなにかけても、断熱層に水が入った瞬間に水が走り、先ほど話していた密着工法のメリットとは真逆なことが起こるわけです。現状では断熱材の下と断熱材の上に2回超速硬化ウレタン防水をかけるという解決法になるのですが、単純に防水自体が断熱性能をもってくれるといいのですけれど（笑）。

多喜茂（たき しげる）

須部 これからは、CLT（クロス・ラミネイティド・ティンバー）をはじめ木の建築がたくさんつくられていくと思うのですが、そのときに断熱であったり、耐火であったり、透明で木の素材感を見せられるものであったり、防水に何か一つでも性能を兼ね備えたものができると、私たちが当たり前と思っていた常識を変えるディテールが生まれるのではないかという気がしています。

赤松 木の素材感を生かすため、トップコートの着色なしでFRP防水を透明なままかけてみたことがありますが、どうしても劣化が起こります。もし、超速硬化ウレタン防水が透明になったら、屋根の開口にガラスをポンと置いてそこに防水を施せば、立上りもサッシも不要になるかもしれないですね。そうしたらすごく画期的（笑）。

須部 まるでファンデーションをのせるように、素材そのものや、建築家が考えたシルエットを素直に表現できるようになるといいですよね。

赤松 今回収録された「アストラムライン新白島駅」（60頁）は、壁や屋根とは全然違うそのものとしての存在を目指したのですが、面として見せて防水性能をもたせようとすると、選択肢は自ずと限られます。3次曲面のデザインにとって超速硬化ウレタン防水が有効なのはもちろん、壁や屋根といったことにとらわれない建築のディテールの一助になる可能性は、そういった性能の向上によりどんどん広がっていくでしょうね。

P113-115の人物写真　撮影：畑拓

From collecting to overflowing

Sube: In recent years, there has seen a shift from asphalt to Ultra fast curing polyurethane waterproofing membrane system for use in the waterproofing of buildings.

Looking back, I think there was a turning point around the year 2000 after the economic bubble burst. At the time, budgets were limited and it was necessary to cut out as much waste as possible. I think Ultra fast curing polyurethane waterproofing membrane system appealed to designers, because it made coping unnecessary and enabled shorter construction time. Another important factor for me personally was that we had a backup system, because the person in charge at the general contractor brought it to our research lab to demonstrate the performance.

Taki: I guess that for a lot of people at the time, polyurethane waterproofing was thought of only as something for coating rooftop "pigeon huts" [HVAC plant] and parapets to create a thin water-resistant film. For reliable waterproofing, people looked to asphalt.

Akamatsu: In the case of a rooftop with asphalt waterproofing, you need to have a parapet riser and covering concrete, so the detail gets more and more complex. But with Ultra fast curing polyurethane waterproofing membrane system, everything fits very simply. The first time we used it at our office, the staff compiled information and case studies of ultra fast curing polyurethane to make a comprehensive evaluation of performance, cost, and design detail.

Sube: I agree with Akamatsu-san that simplicity is a big factor.

The waterproofing method we were taught was complex, with concrete covering on the waterproof layer. Without any clear explanation, we were taught to make the parapet riser at least 600 mm, like this was holy scripture. You put a concrete "chin" on the parapet and protected it with dry board or a wet protective material. Then, you set up overflow pipes at a certain pitch, to collect water and then let it overflow. With all this complexity, however, construction management gets difficult, and with deterioration over time, one thing or another will inevitably fail.

In the old days, Japanese houses had an inubashiri, or berm, running around the house under the eaves to deal with water dripping off the roof. The basic idea was to let the water overflow from the roof. For the people inside the house, it's safer and more secure. With Ultra fast curing polyurethane waterproofing membrane system, this same concept is now possible even with flat roofs, and this is one reason that designers have started using this type of waterproofing.

Enabling unimagined design potential

Taki: Take FRP [fiberglass-reinforced plastic] waterproofing for example. When I started working, it was reliable enough, but after about 15 years the edges of the coping tend to become attached, and when water starts to pass from there into the waterproof layer, you don't know where it gets to. With Ultra fast curing polyurethane waterproofing membrane system, though, a liquid agent is sprayed directly onto a concrete surface using a special machine. The polyurethane adheres strongly to the surface. In extreme cases, pools of water will form on the surface, but not water gets in. So, even for a flat roof with riser, when water overflows from the roof, the building will be protected, because no water will penetrate.

These days, unexpected torrential downpours of rain are a problem, but overflow pipes are only designed to handle so much flow. Touching on what Sube-san said earlier about overflowing, Multi-component ultra fast curing polyurethane waterproofing membrane system can handle massive, unexpected quantities of rain. So it's well suited to the times. Of course, it's essential to get the relationship between levels right, so that water flows off before it gets to stairway openings or entranceways.

Sube: Previously, we had to first create a perfect structure, and then make the holes for overflow. In terms of detail, this new way is certainly safer. The polyurethane adheres well to concrete, metal or any other kind of material, and there's no need to make the concrete "chin" on the parapet at the end.

As a result, the traditional 600 mm parapet, can

be reduced to around 100 or 50 mm, and the saved space can be used as extra living space for the occupants of each floor. From our point of view as designers, this is a very good thing.

Akamatsu: In the design of public school buildings, it is important to minimize ceiling height to keep down total cost, but at the same time you want to maximize usable internal space. The fact that we can reduce the parapet height helps save space and money. With large-footprint buildings, you can also save a substantial amount on concrete.

With the previous method, there were many necessary steps that had to be taken in order. Now, with fewer steps, there are fewer things that can go wrong.

Sube: Without the need for covering concrete, the load conditions in the event of an earthquake will be completely different. As a result, piles can be smaller, pillars can be slimmer, beams can be smaller, etc. In terms of VE (value engineering), this results in higher structural value, and also offers advantages of safety and space-saving. For an earthquake-prone country like Japan, this is a big plus.

A simpler system enables faster problem-solving

Taki: When I started at the company, polyurethane waterproofing was used mostly in combination with rubberized asphalt. There are many kinds of waterproofing techniques, like stainless steel waterproofing, FRP waterproofing, sheet waterproofing, and asphalt waterproofing, but since they all involve laying a membrane to block water, gaps tend to occur in the waterproof layer. This means that as soon as water gets through from any point, you never know where the water will emerge, and there's always a time lag too.

In contrast, with Multi-component ultra fast curing polyurethane waterproofing membrane system, the polyurethane adheres completely to the concrete or other construction surface, so typically once you find a point that needs repair, you only need to deal with that point, because all other points remain perfectly sealed. Since the method is so simple, even if water does happen to penetrate, it is a quick and easy matter to find the cause.

For me, this is the most important point that distinguishes this method so dramatically with the previous approach. Ultimately, what I care about more than the waterproofing is the state of the building, particularly the concrete surface where waterproofing is applied and whether there is laitance formation.

Sube: The waterproofing makers give a 10-year warranty, which gives peace of mind both to architects, owners, and building contractors. For owners, this guarantee provides a strong basis for choosing polyurethane waterproofing, along with the extra space it allows.

If I think about how waterproofing will be 10 years from now based on the current state of renovation, I would predict that urethane waterproofing will replace other methods.

Taki: In many current renovation projects, Multi-component ultra fast curing polyurethane waterproofing membrane system is applied over the covering concrete of the existing asphalt waterproofing.

Sube: Even if asphalt waterproofing is used for another 10 years, as soon as a renovation is done, the waterproofing will be redone with polyurethane and will continue to work for a long period thereafter.

Another thing is that heating is necessary with asphalt waterproofing. The work is smelly and there's also a risk of fire. Ultra fast curing polyurethane doesn't have these issues, so it's safer for contractors and generally they are happy to cooperate in using it.

Various factors have conspired to favor the use of polyurethane since 2000, such as the state of the economy and construction industry, the demands and preferences of architects, and the increasing number of renovation projects.

Detailing with Multi-component Ultra Fast Curing Polyurethane Waterproofing Membrane System

Akamatsu: From the design viewpoint, the biggest difference is in the connecting parts.

For example, with asphalt waterproofing, water tends to leak through the ends of the connecting parts. After being assured of the absolute reliability of stainless steel waterproofing that we used, I was shocked to see that cracks had formed due to fatigue in the seamless welds of the steel. On the other hand, with Ultra fast curing polyurethane waterproofing membrane system, no water gets into the waterproof layer because even the edges are completely sealed by the polyurethane.

Sube: Sheet waterproofing was often used in cases of tight-fitting, intricate architectural designs that we used to see in magazines when we were young.

Akamatsu: Even in sheet waterproofing, the weak point tends to be at the internal corner of the riser.

Sube: Multi-component ultra fast curing polyurethane waterproofing membrane system is not a solid product. It's delivered to the site as a liquid and then applied by spraying, to create a huge seamless space, like an FRP bath tub. In this sense, it's a very different concept of waterproofing.

Akamatsu: The Multi-component ultra fast curing polyurethane waterproofing membrane system is secure in the sense that no water gets in below the layer, but the connecting parts remain essential. As we were saying, more so than the waterproofing layer, water tends to get in through the seals of window frames.

Sube: On this point, it's a good thing that a variety of case studies have been put together.

In my case, to prevent water getting inside, I put stainless steel or other metal at the front of the sash, and in addition, on the indoor side behind the sash, I put a riser to ensure complete waterproofing. Outside, I tend to use a dry area such as a wooden deck, while indoors I often use a raised floor or other feature to create a flat surface.

Taki: Everyone has their own methods, and at the very least some kind of rule. Since I don't want water to slowly seep in, even if the seal is damaged, I always raise the seal below the sash by 2 cm. And even with polyurethane waterproofing, the slope should be 1/50 in my view.

Sube: Some say, a slope of less than 1/100 is no good, so the gradient value needs to be considered.

Akamatsu: Basically, no water should collect. When dust or fallen leaves contain water, a gradient of 1/100 will not allow water to flow, resulting in a puddle. If viewed from above, the impression is untidy, so I use a gradient steep enough to ensure that water always flows to some degree. If debris collects at the drain, it's just a matter of cleaning it. Even if something happens, it will always be easy to see the problem and deal with it.

Greater ease-of-use for designers and builders

Taki: It was only a little over 10 years ago that Multi-component ultra fast curing polyurethane waterproofing membrane system emerged on the market. Although it has made design simpler and building easier, there's still room for improvement in the design of the waterproofing itself. The texture of the top coat applied to the surface is currently glossy, but I often wish that a mortar or concrete-like matte texture were available.

Sube: I occasionally see mortar waterproofing, and that texture is certainly attractive. There are impregnated repair materials, and it might be interesting if something similar were available for Ultra fast curing polyurethane waterproofing membrane system.

One thing I'm concerned about is how to eliminate construction mistakes. Asphalt waterproofing is black, so it is obvious whether it has been applied or not. However, spraying Ultra fast curing polyurethane waterproofing membrane system is done by workers, and it may not always be easy to verify whether or not the worker has sprayed an area or part. This thought is very scary for me. To prevent this, it would be good to use polyurethane of a totally different color to the underlying concrete, so that unsprayed parts and areas are visible at a glance. It would be even better if the color gradually changed over time to assimilate with that of the concrete.

Taki: Speaking of the human element, there's an issue of education and training for the people handling the urethane. Up to now we haven't used the technology on very many projects, so all of us, designers and builders, have studied the method thoroughly. As the method becomes more common and widespread and accepted as safe and secure, only that aspect of the method will tend to be highlighted. I'm a little worried that the important elements of this construction technique and the preliminary conditions will be neglected.

Akamatsu: The impact of heat on metal, concrete, and other materials will vary. Most notably, metals expand and contract. So, variations in adhesive strength with different materials is a subject that requires study.

Sube: I would like to see how close the coating layer adheres to the material, and understand how different materials and environments affect performance. We need some concrete data available on these kinds of questions.

Taki: At the same time, we have to assume that we won't be constructing everything from the ground up in the future. So, the appropriate maintenance method for a particular place will gradually be understood—for example, there is difference between a place exposed to a lot of sunlight, and one that is not exposed at all.

The future of Multi-component Ultra Fast Curing Polyurethane Waterproofing Membrane System

Taki: Now that we are clear about the reliability of Ultra fast curing polyurethane waterproofing membrane system, the next step is that other functions will be required in addition to waterproofing, such as fire resistance for external walls, or when a building is completely coated.

A particular challenge we are facing is thermal insulation. When we want to use undressed concrete indoors, external insulation is needed. However much polyurethane waterproofing is applied to the insulation, the moment water gets into the insulation layer it will spread, resulting in the exact opposite of the adhesive effectiveness we discussed earlier. At present, the solution is to apply the Ultra fast curing polyurethane waterproofing membrane system twice, once under the thermal insulation material and once over it. It would also be helpful if the waterproofing polyurethane itself were a good thermal insulator (laughs).

Sube: I imagine that in the years ahead we'll see a lot more CLT (cross-laminated timber) and other forms of wood construction. At this time, if the waterproofing can provide some extra functionality—even one of thermal insulation, fire resistance, or transparency to enable the texture of wood to show through—this would greatly expand the usability of urethane and truly change the common perception about it.

Akamatsu: In order to take advantage of the natural look of wood, I've tried to use FRP waterproofing transparently, as it is, without the coloring of a top coat, but there was no way to stop deterioration over time. If Ultra fast curing polyurethane waterproofing membrane system is available as a transparent formula, we could simply fit glass to openings in the roof and apply waterproofing, without any need to use risers or sashes. That would be very exciting (laughs).

Sube: It would be nice if architects could express the natural qualities of materials and the shapes they invent, like applying foundation to a face.

Akamatsu: For the Shin-hakushima station on the Astram line, which we recently documented, we aimed at creating a feel completely unlike the familiar one created by walls and roof, but in trying to create a curved surface that is waterproof, the possibilities are naturally quite limited. For 3D curvilinear design, Ultra fast curing polyurethane waterproofing membrane system is very effective, and I really feel that its potential in helping architects to fashion buildings that depart from the conventional spatial concept of four walls and a roof will grow and expand significantly in the years ahead.

インタビュー

超速硬化ウレタン複合防水の現在

ウレタン防水の
パイオニアである、
ダイフレックス・営業推進チームの
石川貴紀氏に
超速硬化ウレタン複合防水の
現状と性能面、
そしてこれからの展望について
お話をうかがった。（編集部）

石川貴紀（いしかわ たかのり）
（ダイフレックス 営業推進チーム）

―――― 今回収録した設計者の鼎談のなかで、2000年以降、超速硬化ウレタン複合防水が広がっていったというお話がありました。

石川 もともとの開発の経緯は、アスファルト防水の押えコンクリートの屋根をVE提案するところから、露出防水で何かいいものがないかという要望を受けて始まりました。弊社の超速硬化ウレタンシステムは1992年に確立され、手塗りウレタンとの複合化をして、今年で15年目を迎えています。

延べ500,000m²超の施工実績がありますが、おかげさまでこれといった大きな不具合は現在まで報告されていません。このことは、当初より弊社の工法についてご理解・ご支援いただいている皆様の期待に応えてきたものだと考えています。

最初の採用事例である「同志社大学寒梅館」（設計：日建設計、施工：大林組）は、2004年に施工し、施工面積は4,300m²ですが、2014年の10年経過点検においても良好な状況が確認されています。

―――― 防水材は機能商品ですから、漏水などの不具合がこれまでにないのは、特筆すべきことですね。

石川 はい。超速硬化ウレタン樹脂は、従来の汎用ウレタンに比べて抜群に性能値が向上していますし、下地との密着性が極めて高いという特徴をフル活用した密着型複合工法が大きく貢献していると思います。

弊社では、コンクリート下地との接着プライマーとして2液反応硬化型エポキシプライマーを使用しています。十分な下地研磨・乾燥養生下では1N/mm²以上の接着強度を発揮します。これは、下地コンクリート材が破壊レベルの強度となります。塗膜層は剥がそうとしても剥がすことは難しく、仮に防水層が損傷を受けた場合もその損傷部から雨水が入って広がらないため、不具合等が生じづらいという特徴があります。

―――― 屋上緑化下での採用事例も多いようですが、防水層の上に緑化基盤を設けてしまうとなかなかメンテナンスができないと思われますが、実質的な耐久性はどの程度を想定されていますでしょうか？

石川 防水層の劣化を促進させる主要因としては、紫外線・熱・水があげられます。緑化用防水仕様では、紫外線・熱劣化について大幅に条件がよくなっていることに加え、耐水・耐薬品に優れるポリウレア樹脂を使用している複合防水工法のため、定期的なメンテナンス等は想定していません。耐久性としては、露出ウレタン防水のリファレンスサービスライフ15年超であると想定しています。（*1）

―――― 性能を確保するうえで、防水施工者に対してのサポート体制などもあるのでしょうか。

石川 超速硬化ウレタン防水が普及する一方で、他の防水材のように施工技能を評価する技能検定（国家検定）はありませんでした。そのため、スプレーウレタン・ウレア工業会（*2）では、より高い施工品質を目指し、厚労省の社内検定制度で認定を受けて、技能検定に準ずる体制を整えました（2013年10月24日厚生労働省認定）。弊社も施工精度の向上を目指し、この検定制度を活用し、支持しています。

―――― より高い施工品質の実現を目指しての取り組みですね。その他、今後設計者などがより安心して採用ができるような試みなどがあればうかがえますか。

石川 弊社では、超速硬化ウレタン防水の技術をさらに広めていくことを目的として、建設技術審査証明書の取得を行いました（2018年10月1日）。（*3）

これは、われわれの超速硬化ウレタン複合防水が、アスファルト防水に代わって、その上を歩行できたり、さまざまな用途に使えるといったことを、有識者の方々に審査していただき、証明書が発行されるというものです。性能が第三者機関によって客観的に証明されることで、今後ますます設計者・発注者の方々も使いやすくなるでしょう。

今後とも良質な材料を提供するとともに、施工の管理をきっちりと行い、リーディングカンパニーとしての責任を果たしていきたいと思っています。

*1 参考：防水層及び、防根層の耐根性能
ポリウレア樹脂PM5000を土中に埋没し、14年後に物性値を測定したところ、各性能値（引裂強度・引張強度・伸び率）は、初期物性の90%程度を保有していた。防水性能を保有する目安の70%を今後も維持できると推測される。（ダイフレックス調べ）

*2 スプレーウレタン・ウレア工業会とは、超速硬化ウレタン材料メーカーと、防水施工会社で組織された工業会（略称：SUK）

*3 建設技術審査証明事業とは、民間において自主的に研究開発された新技術を社会に役立てる目的で、建設大臣告示に基づいて平成13年1月10日に創設した事業

Interview

Current Status of the Multi-component Ultra Fast Curing Polyurethane Waterproofing Membrane Systems

We interviewed Takanori Ishikawa of the Sales Promotion Team in Dyflex, the pioneer in polyurethane waterproofing membrane system, about current status and performances of the Multi-component ultra fast curing polyurethane waterproofing membrane systems and future prospects. (Editor)

——— From what I remember, there was a talk on how the Multi-component ultra fast curing polyurethane waterproofing membrane system became popular rapidly after 2000 in the recorded three-person talk.

Ishikawa: The development of the System began with making value engineering suggestions of the protective concrete layer of asphalt waterproofing in response to requests for a decent material for exposed aggregate finish. Our Ultra fast curing polyurethane waterproofing membrane system was established in 1992 and it is our 15th year since it was combined with hand-coating polyurethane.

Our product has been used to work more than 500,000m², and luckily, no major defects have been reported so far. I believe that this is the result of continuously meeting the expectations of our customers who have been very understanding and supportive of our method from the beginning.

The first application example "Doshisha University Kambaikan" (Designed by: Nikken Sekkei Constructed by: Obayashi Corporation) was constructed in 2004. The total worked area of 4,300m² was still in good condition in 2014, even after 10 years since completion.

——— Waterproofing material is a functional product. It is noteworthy that no defects like water leak have been reported.

Ishikawa: Yes, definitely. The performance of the ultra fast curing polyurethane resin has drastically improved as compared to the old general-purpose urethane. I think that the adhesion-based composite method making full use of the property of excellent adhesion to foundation is making a major contribution.

We are using the two-component reaction-cured epoxy primer for adhesive primer to adhere the material to concrete foundation. It can generate adhesive strength of more than 1N/mm² with sufficient foundation polishing and dry curing. This is equivalent to the strength which can destroy the foundation concrete. The membrane layer can hardly be removed, and defects are rare since it still prevents rainwater from getting in and spreading, even if the waterproof layer has been damaged.

——— I see many applications to rooftop greens, but I believe that it is difficult to maintain when greening base is installed on top of a waterproof layer. What is the estimate for the substantial durability?

Ishikawa: Ultraviolet rays, heat and water are the major causes of waterproof layer degradation. The specification of waterproofing for greens does not expect periodic maintenance as major improvements have been made to resist ultraviolet rays and heat, and it uses the composite waterproofing method with polyurea resins which are excellent in water resistance and chemical resistance. We estimate the Reference Service Life of exposed polyurethane waterproofing to be durable for over 15 years. (*1)

——— Is there any support system for waterproofing engineers in assuring performances?

Ishikawa: While the Ultra fast curing polyurethane waterproofing membrane system was becoming widespread, there was no technology certification (national certification) unlike other waterproofing materials. The Spray Urethane & Urea Industrial Association (*2) has received an approval from the in-house certification system of the Ministry of Health, Labour and Welfare and organized a system which conforms to the technology certification in the aim of achieving better work quality (approved by the Ministry of Health, Labour and Welfare on October 24, 2013). We are supporting this system by using this certification system in order to improve the precision of our work as well.

——— I see, it is certainly the activity for realizing better work quality. Could you tell us if there are any other activities for allowing designers to use the product with ease?

Ishikawa: We have acquired the Construction Technology Review Certification for the purpose of popularizing the technology of Ultra fast curing polyurethane waterproofing membrane system and the certificate was issued on October 1, 2018. (*3) In this review, experts examine and issue a certificate proving that our Multi-component ultra fast curing polyurethane waterproofing membrane system can be used for concrete for sidewalk and other purposes instead of asphalt waterproofing. With a proof of excellent performances issued by a third party organization from an objective point of view, I am sure that this will make it even more easier for designers and our customers to use our product. We will continue to fulfill the responsibilities as a leading company by providing quality materials and managing works thoroughly.

*1 Reference: Waterproof layer and the anti-root performance of the root-proof layer
Measuring the physical property value of the PM5000 polyurea resin buried underground 14 years later, each performance value (tear strength/tensile strength/elongation rate) maintained 90% of the initial physical property. It is estimated that 70%, the approximate percentage for maintaining a waterproof performance, can be maintained continuously. (according to a survey by Dyflex)

*2 The Spray Urethane & Urea Industrial Association is an industrial association organized with manufacturers of the Ultra Fast Curing Polyurethane Material and waterproofing work companies (abbreviation: SUK).

*3 Construction Technology Review Certification Project is a project launched on January 10, 2001 in accordance with the Minister of Construction's notice for the purpose of applying new technology developed voluntarily in private companies to social projects.

編集協力者　略歴（五十音順）
Contributing Editors　Profile

赤松佳珠子（あかまつ かずこ）
1968年　東京都生まれ
1990年　日本女子大学家政学部住居学科卒業
1990年　シーラカンス（のち、C+A、CAtに改組）
2002年　C+Aパートナー
2013年　法政大学准教授
現　在　CAtパートナー、法政大学教授、神戸芸術工科大学非常勤講師

須部恭浩（すべ やすひろ）
1972年　神奈川県生まれ
1995年　明治大学理工学部建築学科卒業
1995年　三菱地所
2001年　三菱地所設計
2009年　同社上海事務所主席代表
現　在　三菱地所設計チーフアーキテクト、明治大学兼任講師

多喜茂（たき しげる）
1966年　滋賀県生まれ
1989年　金沢工業大学建築学科卒業
1991年　同大学院修士課程修了
1991年　日建設計
現　在　日建設計設計主管

Kazuko AKAMATSU
1968   Born in Tokyo
1990   Graduated from Department of Housing, Faculty of Home Economics, Japan Women's University
1990   Coelacanth
1998   Reorganized Coelacanth and Associates（C+A）
2002   Partner of C+A
2005   Reorganized office into CAt
2013   Associate professor at Hosei University
Current   CAt Partner, and Professor at Hosei University, lecture at Kobe Design University

Yasuhiro SUBE
1968   Born in Kanagawa
1995   Graduated from Department of Architecture, Meiji University
1995   Mitsubishi Estate Co., Ltd.
2001   Mitsubishi Jisho Sekkei Inc.
2009   Company's Shanghai office Representative
Current   Chief Architect of Mitsubishi Jisho Sekkei Inc., lecture at Meiji University

Shigeru TAKI
1966   Born in Shiga
1989   Graduated from Department of Architecture, Kanazawa Institute of Technology
1991   Master's Course of Architecture, Kanazawa Institute of Technology
1991   Nikken Sekkei Ltd
Current   Associate Architect of Nikken Sekkei Ltd

防水デザインの現在　超速硬化ウレタン複合防水とディテール
2019年 7 月10日　第 1 版 発　行
2021年11月10日　第 1 版 第 3 刷

　　　　　　　　　編　者　株式会社　彰　国　社
著作権者と　　　　発行者　下　出　雅　徳
の協定によ　　　　発行所　株式会社　彰　国　社
り検印省略
　　　　　　　　　162-0067　東京都新宿区富久町8-21

　自然科学書協会会員
　工学書協会会員　　電話　03-3359-3231（大代表）
Printed in Japan　　振替口座　00160-2-173401
Ⓒ 彰国社　2019年　　　　　印刷：真興社　製本：誠幸堂
ISBN 978-4-395-32140-7　C3052　　http://www.shokokusha.co.jp

本書の内容の一部あるいは全部を、無断で複写（コピー）、複製、および磁気または光記録媒体等への入力を禁止します。許諾については小社あてご照会ください。

本書は、2018年12月に「ディテール別冊」として刊行しましたが、このたび、単行本として新たに刊行しました。